I0100575

Korean Democracy in Transition

A Rational Blueprint for Developing Societies

HeeMin Kim

THE UNIVERSITY PRESS OF KENTUCKY

An earlier version of chapter 3 was published as "Rational Choice Theory and Third World Politics: A Case Study of the 1990 Party Merger in Korea," in *Comparative Politics* 30 (1997): 83–100. An earlier version of chapter 4 was published as "A Theory of Government-Driven Democratization: The Case of Korea," in *World Affairs* 156 (1994): 130–140.

The University Press of Kentucky

Scholarly publisher for the Commonwealth,
serving Bellarmine University, Berea College, Centre College of Kentucky, Eastern Kentucky University, The Filson Historical Society, Georgetown College, Kentucky Historical Society, Kentucky State University, Morehead State University, Murray State University, Northern Kentucky University, Transylvania University, University of Kentucky, University of Louisville, and Western Kentucky University.

Editorial and Sales Offices: The University Press of Kentucky
663 South Limestone Street, Lexington, Kentucky 40508-4008
www.kentuckypress.com

15 14 13 12 11 5 4 3 2 1

Library of Congress Cataloging-in-Publication Data

Kim, HeeMin.
Korean democracy in transition : a rational blueprint for developing societies / HeeMin Kim.
p. cm. — (Asia in the new millennium)
Includes bibliographical references and index.
ISBN 978-0-8131-2994-5 (hardcover : alk. paper) — ISBN 978-0-8131-2995-2 (ebk.)
1. Democracy—Korea (South)—History. 2. Democratization—Korea (South)—History. 3. Korea (South)—Politics and government—1960-1988. 4. Korea (South)—Politics and government—1988-2002. 5. Korea (South)—Politics and government—2002- I. Title.
JQ1729.A15K534 2011
320.95195—dc23 2011019761

This book is printed on acid-free paper meeting the requirements of the American National Standard for Permanence in Paper for Printed Library Materials.

Manufactured in the United States of America.

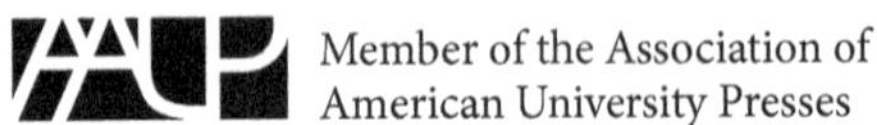

To my mother, Gyung Duk Lee,
whose prayer seems to be working,
and to my wife, Yun, and my children,
Sujin and Sungshik (Patrick) Kim,
who have been so patient with me
over many years.

Contents

Illustrations

Figures

Tables

Acknowledgments

This book has been developed over the period of almost two decades. Because individual chapters were circulated and were presented as papers at various conferences, they have been exposed to numerous critics. As a result, I know that I am intellectually indebted to so many people, but am not sure to whom and for what. I deeply regret that I am unable to list them all here.

Obviously Jun Young Choi of Inha University in Korea, who was a graduate student at Florida State University when several chapters of this book were written as papers, deserves credit for his assistance, comments, and criticisms. Compiling scattered ideas and papers into a book format was done while I was visiting Hankuk University of Foreign Studies in Seoul, Korea, in 2009.

This book project was supported by a Senior Research Grant Program from the Fulbright Foundation, an Advanced Research Grant from the Korea Foundation, and a sabbatical leave from Florida State University. The author retains full responsibility for all content herein, and this project's analyses and conclusions may not necessarily represent the views of the foundations, the university, or any other organization.

Abbreviations

DJP	Democratic Justice Party
DLP	Democratic Liberal Party
DP	Democratic Party
GNP	Grand National Party
IAEA	International Atomic Energy Agency
MMD	Multimember Districts
NCNP	National Conference for New Politics
NDRP	New Democratic Republican Party
NKP	New Korea Party
NMDP	New Millennium Democratic Party
NPP	New Party by the People
PBE	Perfect Bayesian Equilibrium
PPD	Party for Peace and Democracy
PR	Proportional Representation
RDP	Reunification Democratic Party
SMD	Single-Member Districts
UDS	Unified Democracy Scores
ULD	United Liberal Democrats
UNP	Unification National Party

1

Rational Choice, Area Expertise, and Democratic Transition in Developing Societies

A Theoretical Framework

Rational choice refers to the application of microeconomic theory to various decision-making situations. It conceives of the individual as a goal-oriented actor who pursues the best available means to a given end (Booth et al. 1993; van Winden 1988). Rational choice theory assumes methodological individualism and purposeful action. According to methodological individualism, social processes and outcomes are the results of individual preferences and choices. Methodological individualism simply reminds us that only people can set goals, determine their preferences, and choose among possible alternatives. Thus, all group choices ultimately must be understood in terms of individual choices. Human action may be interpreted as directed toward attaining certain goals. People act for certain purposes, and we must understand these purposes in order to explain their actions (Ordeshook 1986).

Rational choice theory has been rigorously applied to many subfields of political science, including American politics, international relations, and, increasingly, comparative politics. The rational choice literature has grown so quickly that it is difficult to name representative writings without doing injustice to many others.

One criticism of the rational choice theory has been the potential lack of usefulness in analyzing political phenomena in developing (or non-Western) areas.[1] Critics object to the application of rational choice to the third world because actors' goals depend on a culturally unique set of values and there is no way of characterizing goals and preferences independently of culture. The model of behavior driven by self-interest is itself culturally specific; it is present in some cultures and absent in others. Critics maintain that the concept of economic rationality applies to the forms of market society that emerged in the West in the early modern period. The rational choice approach is further criticized for ignoring traditions and norms of communities and collectivities by paying attention solely to the self-interest of individuals, even though collective norms are fundamental social factors in still traditional societies (Geertz 1971; Polanyi 1957; Cheng and Tallian 1995).

Another ongoing debate is about the usefulness of rational choice theory in analyzing particular real-world situations. The rational choice school has been known for its ability to develop general theories. With its methodological sophistication, it has developed prominent theories with many testable hypotheses, but according to its critics, this school has paid little attention to individual and real-world political events. Critics point to the abstract and logical character of game theory, but do so in order to condemn it. The failures of rational choice theory, Green and Shapiro declare, are "rooted in the aspiration of rational choice theorists to come up with universal theories of politics." The result, they argue, is a preoccupation with theory development, accompanied by a striking "paucity of empirical application." Research "becomes theory driven rather than problem driven"; its purpose is "to save or vindicate some variant of rational choice theory, rather than to account for . . . political phenomena" (Green and Shapiro 1994). These criticisms of rational choice theory led to the "rational choice vs. area studies" debate in political science (see, for example, Bates 1997a; Bates 1997b; Johnson 1997; and Lustick 1997).

In this book, I view the democratic transition in Korea as a succession of events (puzzles, problems, and so on). I also view a limited number of political elites as main participants in these events. Obviously, the democratic transition in any country cannot be explained solely by an elite or mass-driven theory. But I argue that elites played an important role in important political events and *manipulated* those events much more so than the masses ever could, and thus, the democratic transition in Korea requires, at least partly, an elite-driven explanation.[2] As I will show throughout this book, political elites' history of personal rivalry (even among democracy movement leaders), desire to win over each other, and attempts to prolong the period of their influence played critical roles in the direction and process of democratic transition in Korea. Elites did not hesitate to take advantage of, or even deepen, existing political cleavages for personal gain (Almond et al. 2006). Huntington's prophetic remarks apply to Korea as well as any other country: "institutions come into existence through negotiations and compromises among political elites calculating their own interests and desires" (Huntington 1984, 212). By applying various rational choice approaches to important political events in Korea, I will show that the concern about the over-emphasis of theory on the part of rational choice theory is over-stated.[3]

Various political "events" I analyze in this book range from the decision of the authoritarian government to open up the political process in 1987 to the presidential impeachment of 2004. I also discuss the latest political events in Korea in the concluding chapter of this book. Readers will notice that I analyze the "international" relationships among the United States, South Korea, and North Korea in chapter 6. I study, in particular, the uncertainty the United States and South Korea have about the real intentions behind the North's gesture of reconciliation (and the uncertainty the North has about America's intentions), utilizing Bayesian models. One may find it odd to see such a chapter in a book about democratic transition in *South* Korea.

Up until the first-ever summit of the two Koreas in 2000, the left half of the ideological spectrum had been "missing" in the political discourse in South Korea, even after the democratic opening in 1987. This was mainly due to the memory of the Korean War (1950–1953) and the existence of the Anti-Communism Law (which, by the way, still exists). Especially during the authoritarian era, just the perception of the "left" could cause imprisonment and even death. Almost all of the post-war political parties in Korea had been right-wing parties with little policy differences among them.

The summit between Kim Dae-jung and Kim Jung-il and subsequent reconciliation at least partly changed the political discourse in South Korea. The existing right-wing parties and political leaders still have not relocated themselves in the traditional left-right dimension (that is, about the appropriate size of government) or social left-right dimension (abortion, gay rights, same sex marriage, etc.). However, a new issue dimension (or labeling) has emerged. After the initial euphoria of the summit and about ten years of reconciliation (which primarily meant the South's economic assistance to the North), the South Korean population is facing (1) a group of progressive leaders/parties favoring continued reconciliation and (2) conservatives with assistance fatigue who are suspicious of the North's real intentions for dealing with the South. In sum, the opening of the relationships between South Korea and North Korea and between the United States and North Korea helped a new issue dimension to emerge, changed the direction of political discourse, and fundamentally reshaped the democratic transition in South Korea. Therefore, these changing relationships must be at the core of any discussion of the subsequent democratic transition in Korea.

In this book, I will also attempt to show that, despite cultural differences, a common set of goals and beliefs may be assumed generally in analyses of political events in any country and therefore ample regularities and events in the third world can be analyzed meaningfully using a rational choice framework. Moreover, what sometimes appears to be the pursuit of a collective norm may be instead a collective pursuit of self-interest, as I will demonstrate in subsequent chapters.

Of course, we must not ignore the cultural differences across different regions of the world. At the same time, we must also not give up applying the whole theoretical tradition of rational choice in developing societies. Culture defines or modifies the set of acceptable strategies and participants' preferences, and thus eventually potential outcomes of many political events. Instead of abandoning the theory itself or redefining its core concepts (e.g., Little 1991), we can first make sure that the set of participants, their preferences, and the strategies they use are *reasonable* in the eyes of area experts whose expertise is being analyzed by the researcher. In reality, this is the way social science research is conducted in many areas.

Thus, it is important in any rational choice analysis to carefully specify the preferences of individual actors—that is, what matters is what goes into the utility functions. This calls for the cooperation and coordination of rational choice theorists and area specialists, rather than the rational choice vs. area study controversy.

2

Kims' Dilemma and the Politics of Rivalry

An Analysis of the Democratic Opening and the 1987 Presidential Election

Two seemingly peculiar events took place in South Korea prior to the presidential election in 1987. In June the governing party candidate, Roh Tae-woo, who was practically assured of a win in an indirect presidential election, agreed to a constitutional amendment that would require a direct election of the president in Korea. It was expected that either one of the two major opposition leaders, Kim Dae-jung or Kim Young-sam would be able to beat Roh Tae-woo, a relative newcomer, in a popular election. However, Kim Dae-jung and Kim Young-sam failed to agree on a single presidential candidacy and both of them ran for the presidency. The result was the unpopular governing party candidate Roh winning the popular election with a plurality of only 36.6 percent of those voting. Kim Young-sam and Kim Dae-jung received 28 and 27 percent respectively.

This chapter attempts to analyze, from the rational choice framework, the seemingly irrational action on both sides—that is, the governing party candidate's agreeing to a direct presidential election and the opposition candidates' failing to take this opportunity to win the presidency. To do so, I need to discuss historical events leading up to the events of 1987.

The Events to Be Analyzed

The eighteen years of authoritarian rule by President Park Chung-hee ended when he was assassinated by his own director of the Korean CIA in 1979. In early 1980, Koreans were cautiously optimistic about the prospect for democracy in Korea. They were dismayed by the assumption of power by Major-General Chun Doo-hwan, the commander of the Military Security Command, through a coup against the higher military command as well as the civilian authority. In October a new constitution was approved by a national referendum. Under the new constitution, Chun Doo-hwan won the presidency in an indirect election without competition in January of 1981.

When he took power, Chun disbanded all the political parties of the previous regime and banned the political activities of all the major political figures. In May 1980 several hundred citizens were killed in the suppression of the Kwangju uprising. Kim Dae-jung, a major opposition leader during the Park regime, was arrested on charges of inciting riots. He was sentenced to death, but his death sentence was later reduced to twenty years in prison.

As the political ban on former politicians was lifted for the most part in 1985, the newly strengthened opposition party began to call for a constitutional revision that would include direct election of the president. Faced with large-scale demonstrations by university students, President Chun implied that there was a possibility of a constitutional revision before the scheduled presidential election of 1987. Throughout 1986, however, the opposition demand for a presidential system of government including direct election of the president paralleled the government proposal of a parliamentary system of government.

As the deadlock between the governing party and the opposition on the issue of constitutional revision continued in early 1987, the opposition party was split as Kim Young-sam, a major opposition figure, announced the formation of a new party, the Reunification Democratic Party (RDP). On April 13, President Chun announced his "grave" decision to suspend debate on constitutional revision, as the opposition was badly split and thus was not a responsible negotiating partner. Student protests escalated.

On June 10, the governing Democratic Justice Party (DJP) formally nominated Roh Tae-woo, a former army general and a classmate of Chun at the Korean Military Academy, as the party's presidential candidate for the scheduled (indirect) presidential election later that year. Roh's nomination was followed by extreme levels of violence on the streets of Korea, with firebombs and tear gas canisters being exchanged by students and police.

On June 29, the governing party candidate, Roh Tae-woo, shocked the nation by announcing his eight-point democratization plan, including direct presidential elections and the restoration of Kim Dae-jung's political rights. After his political rights were restored, Kim Dae-jung became an advisor to the opposition Reunification Democratic Party, of which Kim Young-sam was the president. After a few meetings in September, the two Kims failed to agree on a single candidacy and each urged the other not to run for president.

On October 27 the new constitution was approved by a national referendum, with 93.3 percent of those voting accepting it. The next day Kim Dae-jung announced his candidacy and formed a new party, the Party for Peace and Democracy (PPD). Now Kim Dae-jung's split with Kim Young-sam was made official. On December 16, the governing party candidate, Roh Tae-woo, won the direct and popular election with 36.6 percent of the votes cast. The newly elected president, Roh Tae-woo, was sworn in on February 25, 1988. It was the first peaceful and orderly transfer of power in the forty-year constitutional history of the Republic of Korea.[1]

From the description of events above, two questions arise about the seemingly irrational actions on the part of both the governing party and the opposition. Mainly, why did the governing party candidate, Roh Tae-woo, agree to a direct election at the risk of losing when the incumbent president, Chun Doo-hwan, had already declared, earlier in that year, that the presidential election would be held under the existing constitution, which provided for the indirect election of the president? Why didn't the two Kims agree on a single candidacy instead of taking the risk of throwing the election away after decades of struggle to end authoritarian rule and military government?

Various explanations for Roh Tae-woo's action have been offered, including "people power" and "the determination of the opposition" (Cotton 1992; Han Sung-joo 1990; Kihl 1988), "attainment of a certain level of economic development which produced a solid core of middle class citizens, some of whom sided with the student demand for democracy" (Cheng and Krause 1991; Cotton 1992; Han Sung-joo 1990; Kihl 1988; Moon 1988), "a world-wide trend toward democracy,"[2] "a desire not to disrupt the hosting of the 1988 Olympic Games" (Cotton 1992; Han Sung-joo 1990), and "the pragmatic attitude of military-turned-politicians" and "the possible U.S. role in preventing the adoption of a military option"

(Han Sung-joo 1990). The two Kims' action has been described as a product of pure greed. Being certain that his turn to assume power had come, each Kim urged the other to pull out of the race (Cotton 1992; Han Sung-joo 1990).

I generally agree with most of the explanations given for the governing party's decision to accept the opposition demand for direct election of the president and the two Kims' decisions not to pull out of the presidential race. The objective of this chapter is not to offer *the* alternative account of the two events in 1987, but to supplement existing ones.

A caveat applies here. Since I discuss personal preferences that cannot be measured in any scientific way, what I offer is a conjecture rather than a proof. How plausible a conjecture it is is for the readers to determine.

Kims' Dilemma

In this chapter, I will first analyze the two Kims' decisions about whether to run for president by building a simple 2×2 matrix game that I will call the Presidential Candidacy Resignation game, or "Kims' Dilemma." Based on the findings of this game, I will make an inference about Roh Tae-woo's decision to agree to the direct election of the president in the last section of this chapter.

In Kims' Dilemma, the players are the two Kims, and each player has two strategies (options) available to him, mainly to stay (to run for president) and to resign (not to run). Since each player has two strategies, there are four possible outcomes of the game, mainly (Stay, Stay), (Stay, Resign), (Resign, Stay), and (Resign, Resign). I make the following assumptions about the Kims' Dilemma game.

Assumption 1. The Presidential Candidacy Resignation game is a symmetric game.

A symmetric game is one that looks the same to both players (Hamburger 1979). In the Kims' Dilemma game, both players (the two Kims) have the same two strategies available to them, namely stay and resign. Also, according to Assumption 1, the two Kims have close enough ordinal preferences that, if they choose the same strategy (say, if they both choose to stay in the race), they get the same (ordinal) outcome (say, their respective second most preferred outcome).[3] Under Assumption 1, what I conclude about one Kim will also be true of the other. Therefore, I will use

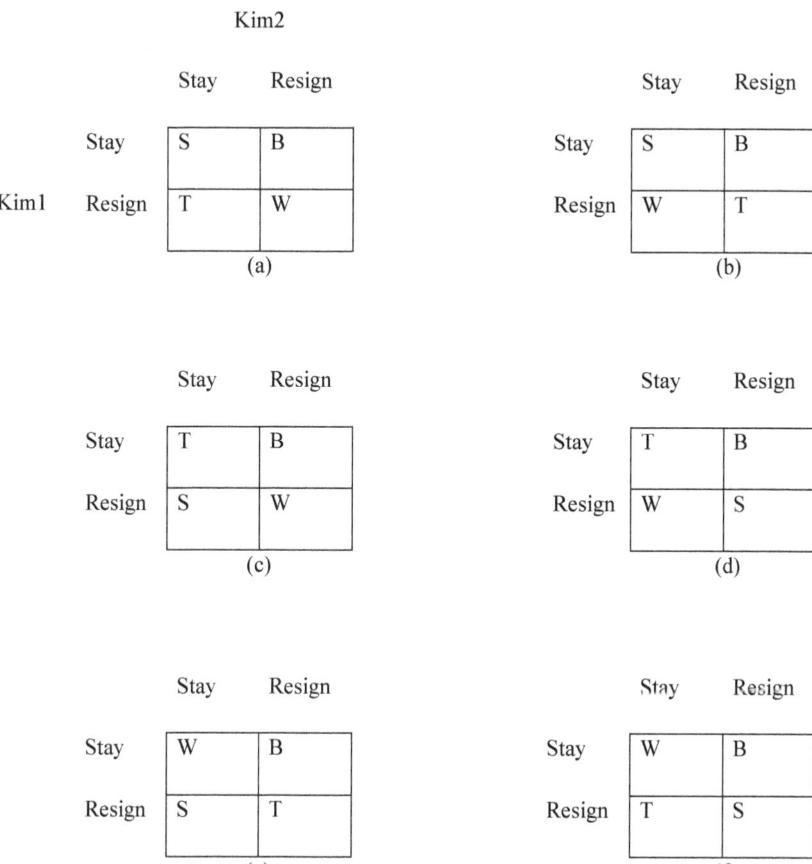

Fig. 2.1. Six possible payoff structures for Kim1, with (Stay, Resign) being the best outcome for him (B = best outcome, S = second best outcome, T = third best outcome, W = worst possible outcome).

only the row-chooser (the player who gets to choose between the two rows in a 2×2 matrix game), whom I will call Kim1, in figure 2.1 from here on.

Assumption 2. Out of four possible outcomes of the Presidential Candidacy Resignation game, Kim1's most preferred outcome is (Stay, Resign). Likewise, Kim2's most preferred outcome is (Resign, Stay).

Kim2 is the column chooser, that is, the player who gets to choose between the two columns in a matrix game (see figure 2.1). Since Kim1's strategy always precedes Kim2's strategy, the (Stay, Resign) outcome means that Kim1 stays in the race while Kim2 drops out. A (Resign, Stay) outcome means that Kim1 pulls out while Kim2 stays in the race. Then Assumption 2 simply states that each Kim's most preferred outcome is that he himself stays in the presidential race (run against Roh Tae-woo) while the other Kim does not run. Given the fact that the two Kims collectively received 55 percent of the total votes eventually cast (meaning there was a good chance to beat Roh if only one Kim should run), and that they were in the race to win the presidency, Assumption 2 is not a strong assumption.

Out of many possible payoff structures (for Kim1) of the 2×2 matrix game, there are only six that satisfy Assumption 2. Figure 2.1 shows all six. In the figure, B, S, T, and W respectively stand for the best outcome (the most preferred outcome), the second best outcome, the third best outcome, and the worst possible outcome to Kim1. All six matrices in figure 2.1 show Kim1's most preferred outcome to be (Stay, Resign) (the upper right corner of the 2×2 matrix), which is exactly what Assumption 2 states. Accepting Assumption 2 as plausible, the next question is: which one of the six in figure 2.1 adequately describes the Presidential Candidacy Resignation game between the two Kims in 1987?

To answer this question, I attempt to compare the expected utilities Kim1 derives from the (Stay, Stay) outcome (the upper left corner of the 2×2 matrix) and the (Resign, Stay) outcome (the lower left corner of the 2×2 matrix). That is, I try to find out, between the outcome of staying in the race along with the other Kim and the outcome of pulling out of race so that the other Kim can face Roh Tae-woo as the only legitimate opposition candidate, which one seemed to be a better outcome to Kim1 at the time the two Kims made their decisions about whether to run or not in 1987.[4]

The expected utility to Kim1 of staying in the race when Kim2 also runs (when the upper left corner of the 2×2 matrix becomes the outcome of the game) can be expressed by the following equation:

Equation 1

$$EU_1 (S,S) = P_{ss/1}[B_{ss/1} - C_{ss/1}] + P_{ss/2}[B_{ss/2} - C_{ss/2}] + P_{ss/3}[B_{ss/3} - C_{ss/3}]$$

where $EU_1 (S,S)$ is the expected utility, to Kim1, of staying in the race, when Kim2 also runs; $P_{ss/1}$, $P_{ss/2}$, and $P_{ss/3}$ are Kim1's expected probabilities of Kim1, Kim2, and Roh Tae-woo each winning the election, respectively (that is, these are Kim1's subjective estimations, at the time he made his decision about whether to run, about the likelihood of each candidate eventually winning the election); $B_{ss/1}$, $B_{ss/2}$, and $B_{ss/3}$ are the benefits to Kim1 when Kim1, Kim2, and Roh Tae-woo each win the election, respectively; and $C_{ss/1}$, $C_{ss/2}$, and $C_{ss/3}$ are the costs to Kim1 when Kim1, Kim2, and Roh win.

There were only three realistically possible outcomes of the 1987 presidential election should both Kims decide to run; namely, wins by Kim Young-sam, Kim Dae-jung, and Roh Tae-woo. There are three combined terms in Equation 1, and they represent these three possible outcomes. Each combined term contains Kim1's estimated probability of a certain candidate's winning and the benefit and the cost to Kim1 when that candidate actually wins. It needs to be noted that, since Equation 1 represents the expected utility to Kim1, all the benefits and the costs in the equation are those to Kim1, and all the expected probabilities are Kim1's subjective estimations.

We may be able to simplify Equation 1 by deleting some of the terms that may not be contributing factors in any meaningful fashion. Take $C_{ss/1}$ for example. This term represents the cost, to Kim1, of winning an election in a race involving the two Kims and Roh Tae-woo. I cannot think of any cost of significant value that Kim1 has to bear (whether Kim1 is Kim Young-sam or Kim Dae-jung) when he beats both the rival Kim and the governing party candidate. Now let us look at $B_{ss/2}$. This is the benefit of losing an election to the rival Kim after campaigning against him. Again, there seem to be no benefits of significant value to Kim1 in this situation. Likewise, $B_{ss/3}$, the benefit of losing an election to Roh Tae-woo, must be negligible. Since the values of these three terms are negligible, we can safely assume that they are zero and ignore them. Then Equation 1 above is reduced to Equation 2 below:

Equation 2

$$EU_1 (S,S) = P_{ss/1}B_{ss/1} - P_{ss/2}C_{ss/2} - P_{ss/3}C_{ss/3}$$

The expected utility, to Kim1, of dropping out of the race, when Kim2 stays in the race (when the lower left corner of the 2×2 matrix becomes the outcome of the game), can be expressed by the following equation:

Equation 3

$$EU_1 (R,S) = P_{rs/2}[B_{rs/2} - C_{rs/2}] + P_{rs/3}[B_{rs/3} - C_{rs/3}]$$

where EU_1 (R,S) is the expected utility, to Kim1, of dropping out of the race (not running for the presidency) so that Kim2 can face Roh Tae-woo in the presidential election; $P_{rs/2}$ and $P_{rs/3}$ are Kim1's expected probabilities of Kim2 and Roh each winning the election, respectively; and $B_{rs/2}$, $C_{rs/2}$ and $B_{rs/3}$, $C_{rs/3}$ are the benefits and costs to Kim1 when Kim2 and Roh Tae-woo each win the election, respectively.

Since Kim1 is not running, there are only two realistically possible outcomes of the presidential election, mainly the win by Kim2 or Roh, and that's why there are only two combined terms in Equation 3. Again, since EU_1 *(R,S)* is the expected utility to Kim1 of not running for president, the two expected probabilities in the equation are Kim1's subjective estimations about the likelihood of Kim2 or Roh winning, and the benefits and costs are those that Kim1 derives from these two outcomes.

Earlier I said I would compare the expected utilities Kim1 derives from (Stay, Stay) outcomes and (Resign, Stay) outcome to figure out which of the six 2×2 matrices in figure 2.1 most adequately describes the Presidential Candidacy Resignation game between the two Kims in 1987. Now we can do exactly that by comparing the probable values of Equation 2 and Equation 3.

As I stated in the first section of this chapter, these equations contain subjective probabilities and the intensity of personal preferences (the values of benefits and costs), which cannot be measured in any scientific way. There are, however, enough known historical events and circumstantial evidence to allow us to make a reasonable conclusion about the values of these equations. I begin with Equation 2—that is, the expected utility of running, knowing that the other Kim is running as well.

The Expected Utility of Running: EU_1 (S,S)

Two terms in Equation 2 deserve special attention, mainly $B_{ss/1}$ (the benefit of winning in a three-way race) and $P_{ss/1}$ (each Kim's assessment about his own chance of winning). After considering these two terms in detail, I will try to evaluate the whole equation at the end of this section.

1. The Spoils of Winning: $B_{ss/1}$

It is commonly said that the two Kims have struggled in the political arena for decades in order to become president. Both actual and psychological benefits of running for and winning the presidency must have been enormous to both Kims for realizing their life-long goals, achieving a sense of power, implementing policies of their own choosing, and so on. In formal terms, they must have attached extremely high value to the term $B_{ss/1}$. The "personal greed" explanation of two Kims' behavior mentioned earlier mainly focuses on this benefit.

2. Miscalculation or Misinformation: $P_{ss/1}$

This term concerns the probability of Kim1 winning even when both Kims run. It is an expected probability (since it is a probability about a future event) as well as a subjective probability (since each Kim assessed the probability of his winning based on the information he gathered using his own information processing system according to his own belief system).

Each Kim seemed to be convinced that he could and in fact would win the election when both Kims ran against the governing party candidate, Roh Tae-woo. Kim Young-sam believed that, with the support of rapidly expanding middle-class voters as well as voters in his native South Kyongsang province, he could handily beat both Roh Tae-woo, a former military general, on his right and Kim Dae-jung, an advocate of mass democracy, on his left. It was sort of a Korean version of the median voter theorem (Black 1958; Downs 1957). An article on Kim Duk-yong, Kim Young-sam's top political aide, revealed that after the election result was declared, Kim Young-sam was so convinced that it was he who had actually won the election, and that Roh Tae-woo's win was the result of a fraud in vote counting, that he contemplated engaging in a campaign to reject the official result of the election. This plan was later abandoned after days of persuasion by his aides (Kim Chang-gi 1992). In short, Kim Young-sam was sure, before the election, that he would win—and after the election, that he had actually won it.

Kim Dae-jung was also convinced that he would win with the overwhelming support of his native Cholla provinces and the urban disaffected. In fact, his strategy (and justification to stay in the race) was "Saja Pilseungron" (the strategy of sure win in the contest of four candidates). According to this strategy, Roh Tae-woo and Kim Young-sam, both from the Kyongsang provinces, would split the votes in those provinces with 7.5 million eligible voters, a fourth candidate by the name of Kim Jong-pil, a former prime minister under Park Chung-hee, would win his native

Chungchong provinces with 2.6 million voters, and Kim Dae-jung would sweep 3.7 million votes in Cholla provinces and finish first in the 11.6 million-vote-strong northern region, which includes the capital city of Seoul.[5]

In a personal interview, a former Kim Dae-jung aide (who wants to remain anonymous) told me that there was no attempt to assess the probability of either Kim Young-sam's or Roh Tae-woo's winning the election because the Kim Dae-jung camp simply believed they would win. In a meeting with his aides on the very day of the election, Kim Dae-jung said he had already won the election and that all that was left to do was to prevent election fraud.

Now let us evaluate the whole equation. That is, we are going to evaluate how attractive an option it was to run for the presidency knowing that the other Kim was also running. From the discussion above, we know that the value of the first combined term in Equation 2 ($P_{ss/1}B_{ss/1}$) is very high (and of course, positive).

Now $C_{ss/2}$ represents the cost to Kim1 when the other Kim wins the election. Besides Kim1's ego being devastated, Kim1 would be considered as the one who should not have run in the first place, which might put him under pressure to retire from politics altogether. $C_{ss/3}$ represents the cost of running when the governing party candidate, Roh Tae-woo, turns out to be the winner (which actually happened). This cost may involve the loss of popularity among the general populace, a certain level of pressure to retire, and potential continuation of authoritarianism in Korea. So the values of these costs seem to be sizable.

However, due to the high value each Kim assigns to $P_{ss/1}$ (his own chance of winning), the values of $P_{ss/2}$ and $P_{ss/3}$ become very low.[6] This makes the second combined term ($-P_{ss/2}C_{ss/2}$) and the third combined term ($-P_{ss/3}C_{ss/3}$) have low negative values. The negative values of the second and third combined terms in Equation 2 are thus more than offset by the first combined term. In short, the choice of running for president even when the other Kim also runs is still a pretty attractive one in the *eyes of each Kim* due to his intense preference for the presidency as well as the extremely generous assessment of his own chance of winning (from the description of the two Kims' behavior above, one may very well conclude that each Kim's subjective probability of his winning the election was dangerously close to 1).

The Expected Utility of Not Running: $EU_1 (R,S)$

Now I turn to Equation 3 and try to assess the expected utility, to each Kim, of not running (dropping out of the race) and letting the other Kim run against Roh Tae-woo. As I did in the previous section, I will consider the terms with greater impacts on the value of Equation 3 first and then evaluate the whole equation.

1. Compensation for Yielding: $B_{rs/2}$

Had one of the two Kims withdrawn "gracefully," he would have become an even more popular figure among the general public for restraining personal desire in the cause of democratization. He also would have been heavily rewarded politically by the other Kim had the latter become the elected president of Korea. Since the president appoints the members of the cabinet and thus controls the executive branch under the presidential system of Korea, the most plausible scenario was that the Kim who withdrew would have been awarded control over the new governing party, and the legislative branch if possible. But this option might not have been as attractive as it sounds since the two Kims had already been either directly or indirectly controlling the major opposition party for almost two decades.

2. The Costs of Not Running: $C_{rs/2}$ and $C_{rs/3}$

Had either of the two Kims decided not to run, he would have had to bear the cost of his decision, and this cost must have been high due to the personal rivalry between Kim Young-sam and Kim Dae-jung and the pressure of regionalism, among other things.

i. Personal Rivalry As I mentioned in the first chapter of this book, political elites' history of personal rivalry, even among democracy movement leaders, played critical roles in the direction and the pace of democratic transition in Korea. The most important rivalry with lasting impact was the one between Kim Young-sam and Kim Dae-jung. The personal rivalry between the two Kims went back to 1968, when Kim Dae-jung was nominated for the position of floor leader of the New Democratic Party, the major opposition party under the Park Chung-hee regime. Kim

Dae-jung's ratification as the new floor leader failed to get the required majority of votes, for he failed to get the support of Kim Young-sam, the previous floor leader of the party. Since Kim Dae-jung's ratification failed, Kim Young-sam was elected as the floor leader for another term (Cho 1993).

The next encounter between the two Kims came at the 1970 national convention of the New Democratic Party. There, Kim Young-sam and Kim Dae-jung, relatively young men in their forties, argued for a generational change in the leadership of the party and sought the party's nomination for the scheduled presidential election of 1971 against the incumbent president, Park Chung-hee.

Kim Young-sam was endorsed by Ryu Jin-san, the influential president of the party, and was widely believed likely to win the nomination. It is said that he had already prepared, before the convention, his victory speech accepting the party's nomination. When the votes were cast and counted, Kim Young-sam received 421 of the 885 total votes cast, Kim Dae-jung received 382 votes, and the remaining 82 votes were invalid votes. This result meant that, although Kim Young-sam came in first, he was 22 votes shy of the simple majority necessary to win the nomination and there would be a second ballot between the two Kims on the very same day.

It turned out that 70 of the 82 invalid votes were blank ballots, a sort of protest vote cast mainly by the supporters of a would-be candidate for the nomination, Lee Chul-seung, who belonged to the same faction as Kim Young-sam and couldn't run because the party's president picked Kim Young-sam to represent that faction in the contest.

After forty minutes of intensive political maneuvering by the two camps, the second ballot was held. To everybody's amazement, the result of the first ballot was reversed and this time it was Kim Dae-jung who came in first, with 458 out of 884 total votes cast. Kim Young-sam received 410 votes and there were 16 invalid votes. This result meant that Kim Dae-jung acquired the party's nomination for the presidency by exceeding the necessary majority by only 15 votes. This result was unexpected even by Kim Dae-jung, who had not prepared an acceptance speech and thus had to speak without a manuscript in front of him.

It was later revealed that Kim Dae-jung made a deal with the loyal supporters of Lee Chul-seung, the would-be candidate, during the forty-minute period between the first and second ballots. Mainly, Kim Dae-jung promised to help Lee get control of the party (in other words, to help him to become the party's new president) in return for Lee's support in the second ballot. It is widely believed that this deal with the Lee supporters was instrumental for Kim Dae-jung's win in the second ballot and, thus, his nomination for the presidency.[7]

The 1970 national convention of the New Democratic Party produced two strong leaders of the opposition. But the nature of the voting outcome there (such as the closeness of the race, the reversal of the results, and the coalition with a third group to win) produced a strong rivalry between the two men. Mainly, each Kim began to perceive the other as a major hurdle to overcome before he could claim an ultimate leadership in the opposition and eventually become the president of the country.

Ever since the two young Kims ran for the party's nomination for the presidency in 1970, they were de facto leaders of the opposition whether they were in or out of party politics. There had been different opposition parties over the years, but the two Kims' predominance within the opposition did not change. The rivalry between Kim Young-sam and Kim Dae-jung intensified as they developed their own followers within the opposition, largely based on their regional origin. Even when the two Kims appeared to cooperate when they found a common enemy in Park Chung-hee and later in Chun Doo-hwan, the struggle between the two factions to expand their power bases within the opposition continued. One example would be the New Korea Democratic Party, in which there was an apparent conflict between the two factions over the distribution of the key positions after the party's national convention in August 1985, although neither Kim was a member of the party at the time.

Several writers have written that the chasm created by the personal rivalry between the two Kims permitted the antidemocratic forces to gain control of events after the assassination of Park Chung-hee in 1979. Mainly, the supporters of Kim Young-sam and the supporters of Kim Dae-jung competed between themselves instead of joining forces, and that (at least partially) contributed to the emergence of the authoritarian Chun Doo-hwan regime and the delay in the transition to democracy (Cotton 1992; Han Dong-yun 1990; Park 1992).

The two Kims' contrasting history of struggle against authoritarian regimes might have added something to the rivalry between them. Since the emergence of the two Kims as major opposition figures, Kim Young-sam remained active in party politics, with sporadic (and forced) breaks.

Therefore, he spent more time as a president of—or as an advisor to—the major opposition parties. Kim Dae-jung, on the other hand, had been forced out of party politics for the most part, and spent time in jail or under house arrest. In 1987, Kim Dae-jung felt he had suffered more than Kim Young-sam in the cause of democracy and thus was a more deserving candidate for the presidency (Han Dong-yun 1990). As far as Kim Young-sam was concerned, Kim Dae-jung had already run, unsuccessfully, for the presidency in 1971 against Park Chung-hee, and it was he (Kim Young-sam) who deserved a shot at the presidency. In sum, the intense rivalry between the two Kims and each Kim's eagerness to prevail over the other made the cost of yielding extremely high.

ii. The Pressure of Regionalism It has been well noted that regionalism is one of the dominant cleavages in Korean politics, if not the most dominant one. In 1987, the emergence of four presidential candidates (including Kim Jong-pil) with four different regional support bases had the effect of deepening the antagonism among different regions. As noted above, both Roh Tae-woo and Kim Young-sam were from the Kyongsang provinces, but strictly speaking, Roh Tae-woo was from North Kyongsang province (with 3.1 million eligible voters) while Kim Young-sam was the favorite son of South Kyongsang province (with 4.4 million eligible voters).

The pressure of regionalism and the potential cost of failing to run was especially real for Kim Dae-jung, who was the native son of the Cholla provinces. The sense of economic deprivation among the people of Cholla caused by regional favoritism during the reigns of Park Chung-hee and Chun Doo-hwan (1961–1987), both from North Kyongsang province, was at its highest point. On top of this long-term economic deprivation came the bloody suppression of the Kwangju uprising in May 1980. The Kwangju uprising, which began as a protest movement against the state of national emergency proclaimed by the Chun Doo-hwan regime, was later suppressed by the special forces unit sent by Chun, resulting in several hundred casualties.

Under these circumstances, Kim Dae-jung, having been the most prominent opposition figure from Cholla provinces under the Park and Chun regimes, having suffered physically and emotionally through repeated jailing and house arrest, and having been sentenced to death on the charge of inciting riots during the Kwangju uprising, was naturally perceived by the people of Cholla as an almost messianic figure who could soothe the sorrow of Cholla. The level of expectation about Kim Dae-jung among the people of Cholla was evidenced by the extent of support he received later in the presidential election. He received 80.9 percent of the total votes cast in North Cholla province, 87.9 percent of the total votes in South Cholla province, and 93.3 percent of the total votes cast in the city of Kwangju. This level of support from a single region has not been surpassed by any candidate in the presidential electoral history of the republic.

Under these circumstances, it was virtually unthinkable for Kim Dae-jung not to run, simply because the cost of pulling out of the race was enormous not only to the region but to Kim Dae-jung himself. Kim Dae-jung's absence from the presidential election would mean that the contest would be between the two native sons of Kyongsang provinces, which, in turn, would mean (to the people of Cholla) the continuation of the past and political, economic, and social domination by Kyongsang provinces. The sense of betrayal and hopelessness that Kim Dae-jung's voluntary withdrawal from the race might produce could last and might eventually hurt Kim Dae-jung's political survival—and his political survival was on the line, partly because of the lack of support he had outside of the Cholla provinces.[8] Betraying the high expectation of the people of Cholla might well mean losing his (only) electoral stronghold, and Kim Dae-jung simply was not ready to bear that cost.

Now let us evaluate the whole equation. That is, we will try to determine how attractive an alternative it was to pull out of the presidential race and let the other Kim face Roh Tae-woo. In Equation 3, $B_{rs/3}$ represents the benefit of not running when the governing party candidate eventually wins the election. It may involve higher popularity for knowing when to step down gracefully. People would say this Kim should have run instead of the other Kim, who just lost the election to Roh Tae-woo. It may prolong his political life and give him another chance to run in 1992. In Korea, however, the future of politics has always been uncertain and politicians tend to discount the future heavily, so that the value of this benefit may not be as high as it sounds.

Then, whatever each Kim's subjective assessments of the chances of the other Kim's win and Roh Tae-woo's win ($P_{rs/2}$ and $P_{rs/3}$) were, the benefits in both the first and second half of the equation ($B_{rs/2}$ and $B_{rs/3}$) are heavily offset, if not outweighed, by the costs in the equation ($C_{rs/2}$ and $C_{rs/3}$). That means the expected utility of not running (the value of Equation 3) was likely to be low, if not negative. In short, not running was not an attractive choice.

Discussion

In the previous section, I attempted to evaluate Equation 2 and Equation 3 based on the circumstantial evidence and known historical facts. From that endeavor, I may be able to establish the following inequality relationship:

$EU_1 (S,S) > EU_1 (R,S)$

That is, the expected utility, to each Kim, of running for president when the other Kim was also running (Equation 2) was greater than the expected utility of not running so that the other Kim could face Roh Tae-woo alone (Equation 3). In other words, running for president even when the fellow opposition leader was also running was simply a more attractive alternative than yielding so that the other could face Roh Tae-woo as the only legitimate opposition in the race. This observation is still a conjecture which cannot be proved since the subjective probabilities and the intensity of personal preferences (in the form of benefits and costs) in the equations cannot be measured in any scientific fashion, although I feel there is enough historical evidence to make my observation a credible one.

The purpose of comparing the expected utilities Kim1 derives from the (Stay, Stay) and (Resign, Stay) outcomes was to figure out which one of six matrices in figure 2.1 adequately describes the Presidential Candidacy Resignation game Kim Young-sam and Kim Dae-jung played in 1987. If my conjecture above (the inequality relationship) is true, then I can successfully eliminate matrices (c), (e), and (f) in figure 2.1 since the expected utility, to Kim1, of the (Stay, Stay) outcome (in other words, the value of Equation 2) is lower than the expected utility of the (Resign, Stay) outcome (the value of Equation 3) in all three matrices. That is, they do not satisfy the inequality relationship above. That leaves us three matrices in figure 2.2 below. One of them precisely describes the Kims' Dilemma game.

A close examination of all three matrices in figure 2.2 reveals the fol-

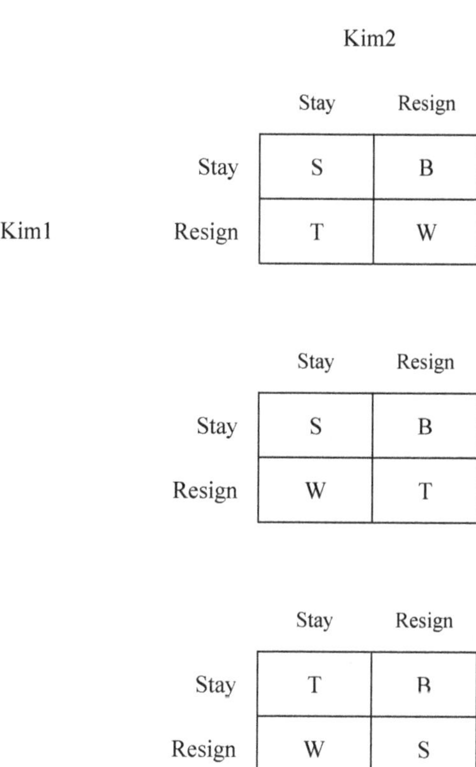

Fig. 2.2. Presidential Candidacy Resignation game ("Kims' Dilemma" game). (Three possible payoff structures for Kim1).

lowing: no matter what Kim2 chooses, Kim1 is always better off choosing "Stay." Let's look at an example. In the matrix at the top, if Kim2 chooses "Stay," Kim1 gets his second best outcome when he chooses "Stay" and his third best outcome when he chooses "Resign." So he's better off when he chooses "Stay." If Kim2 chooses "Resign," Kim1 gets his best possible outcome when he chooses "Stay" and the worst possible outcome when he chooses "Resign." Therefore, no matter what Kim2 chooses, Kim1 is better off by choosing "Stay." It is easy to see that the same is true for the remaining two matrices in figure 2.2.

"No matter what your opponent chooses, you are strictly better off by choosing a certain strategy." That's exactly the definition of what game theorists call a "dominant strategy" (Hamburger 1979; Ordeshook 1986). Then

"Stay" was the dominant strategy for Kim1 in all three matrices in figure 2.2 and thus in the Presidential Candidacy Resignation game. Since Kims' Dilemma is a symmetric game (Assumption 1), what is true about Kim1 is also true about Kim2. So, "Stay" was the dominant strategy for Kim2 as well.

In any game situation, one must use a dominant strategy if he has one since, by definition, he cannot possibly do better by choosing something else. When both players have dominant strategies, they both will choose them and the resulting outcome is "the dominant strategy equilibrium," an outcome that is most stable and thus most predictable.

From the game-theoretic point of view, Kim Young-sam's and Kim Dae-jung's inability to agree on a single candidacy in 1987 was hardly surprising. They simply chose their dominant strategy of "Stay," which was perfectly rational given their expected utility calculations. This may well explain why there was no attempt to resume the discussion about the possible compromise between the two Kims after their initial meeting of September 30, when they failed to agree. They both had the dominant strategy of "Stay," that is, running for president no matter what the other Kim did, and thus they didn't have reason to talk. Both Kims running for the presidency was a "dominant strategy equilibrium."

The "[irrational] personal greed" explanation of the two Kims' actions focuses on the benefit of running for president ($B_{ss/1}$ in Equation 2) and neglects each candidate's assessment of his chance of being elected ($P_{ss/1}$ in Equation 2) and the costs of not running ($C_{rs/2}$ and $C_{rs/3}$ in Equation 3). As we saw in the previous section, running for president was the dominant strategy for both Kims not only because the benefit of running was great, but also because the subjective probability of winning and the costs of not running were also high. The Kims' Dilemma model in this chapter gives a complete description of why the two Kims failed to agree on a single candidacy, even at the risk of throwing the election away.

The analysis of the Kims' Dilemma game above may help explain another puzzle posed in the introduction of this chapter. Mainly, why did Roh Tae-woo (or Chun Doo-hwan, depending upon whom you believe) accept the opposition demand for the direct and popular election of the president at the risk of losing the election? If the governing party had enough information about the two Kims' likely assessments of their own electability and intensity of preferences in the form of benefits and costs, it would not be difficult to predict the outcome of the Kims' Dilemma game (which, after all, had a dominant strategy equilibrium). Given the outcome of the Kims' Dilemma game, Roh Tae-woo's decision, in June of 1987, to allow the direct presidential election was not as risky a strategy as it was originally portrayed by politicians, journalists, and the students of Korean politics, as long as the Kims' Dilemma game was actually played later in that year. We need to note that Roh Tae-woo announced his eight-point democratization plan on June 29, 1987, including direct presidential election *and amnesty for Kim Dae-jung and the restoration of his political rights.* Thus, we have good reason to suspect that Kim Dae-jung's political rights were restored *not despite Roh Tae-woo's decision to allow direct presidential elections, but because of it,* so that he could run (in other words, so that Kims' Dilemma could be played) later in that year.

Conventional approaches to the two events that I discuss in this chapter explain them in chronological order. That is, they say such and such factors affected Roh Tae-woo's decision in June, and pure greed on the part of the two Kims explains their failure to rally behind a single presidential candidacy later in that year. What I suggest in this chapter is that these two events of 1987 are necessarily interrelated and should not be seen as two separate and unrelated decisions. Rational politicians can look ahead, and therefore, sometimes backward induction (analyzing events in counter-chronological order to see the effect of anticipated events on earlier decisions) is necessary.

Then we can view the two events of 1987 as a single game, in which Roh/Chun made the first move and the two Kims the second, as in figure 2.3. If Roh/Chun can anticipate the two Kims' later decisions, then they

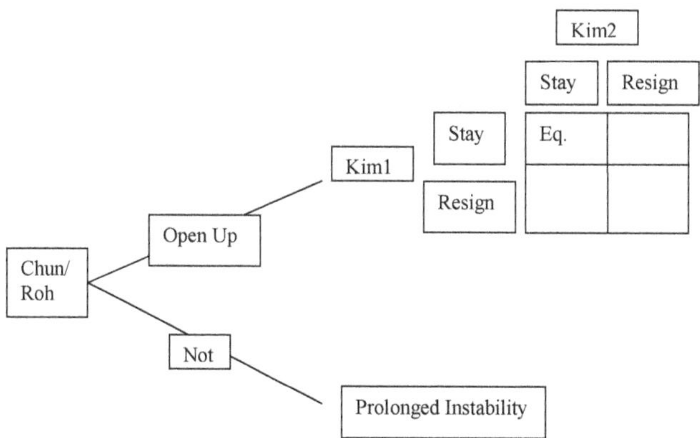

Fig. 2.3. Democratic opening and "Kims' Dilemma" as a single sequential game.

should take advantage of available information when they make their decision.

I will finish this chapter by citing interesting statistics. In the previous section, I argued that the personal rivalry between Kim Young-sam and Kim Dae-jung, along with the pressure of regionalism, made the cost of not running extremely high. If the voting pattern of major constituencies can be an indicator of a candidate's preferences, the following statistics are illuminating. In Kim Young-sam's native province of South Kyongsang, he finished first with 50.3 percent of the total votes cast. The second-place finish went to the governing party candidate, Roh Tae-woo, who received 40.4 percent, and Kim Dae-jung received only 4.4 percent of the total votes.

In Kim Dae-jung's native Cholla provinces, we see quite a different picture. In North Cholla province, Kim Dae-jung received 80.9 percent of the total votes, Roh Tae-woo finished second with 13.7 percent, and Kim Young-sam received only 1.4 percent. The pattern is similar in South Cholla province, where Kim Dae-jung, Roh Tae-woo, and Kim Young-sam received 87.9 percent, 7.9 percent, and 1.1 percent, respectively. And in the city of Kwangju, Kim Dae-jung swept in with 93.3 percent, Roh Tae-woo was second again with 4.5 percent, and Kim Dae-jung's personal rival, Kim Young-sam, finished last with 0.4 percent! The result is startling especially when we consider that both Kim Dae-jung and Kim Young-sam, as opposition leaders, fought together for decades to end military rule in Korea, and Roh Tae-woo was a former army general who, in 1980, was a core member (along with Chun Doo-hwan) of a group of young generals who successfully staged a military coup and later decided to use the army to suppress the Kwangju uprising, although there is no evidence suggesting Roh's direct involvement in this decision.

Some of the evidences I presented in this chapter cannot be measured scientifically and are largely based on conjectures. As I emphasized in chapter 1, what is important is whether the Korea specialists would find them "reasonable." Much of my evidence came directly from the two Kims' camps, and some information about their personal rivalry is common knowledge. I am cautiously optimistic that Korea specialists would find the evidences I present in this chapter reasonable and believable.

3

Building a New Party System

The 1990 Party Merger

The thirteenth national assembly election in Korea, held in 1988 and governed by the new electoral law enacted earlier that year, produced a four-party system.[1] These four parties were the governing DJP and the RDP, the PPD, and the New Democratic Republican Party (NDRP). In January 1990 the DJP, NDRP, and RDP merged to form the Democratic Liberal Party (DLP) and effectively created a two-party system. The PPD was excluded from this new coalition.

The merger of the DJP, NDRP, and RDP is puzzling for at least two reasons. First, these parties had very different historical roots, and thus indulging in the idea of merging them seemed to be preposterous at best. Second, both experts and laymen mentioned other merger scenarios that seemed to make more sense than the actual outcome. For example, a DJP-NDRP coalition (without the RDP) would have secured a simple majority of seats in the national assembly. Kim Jong-pil and many members of the NDRP belonged to power elites under Park Chung-hee's authoritarian regime and had military backgrounds. Although Kim Jong-pil was ostracized along with the two other Kims by Chun Doo-hwan, the NDRP and the governing DJP (with a similar military background) still shared a homogeneous conservative political orientation. From 1987, some younger members of the national assembly had called for a merger between the RDP and PPD, the traditional liberal opposition parties, to form a strong unified opposition (Kim and Kim 1990). The RDP-PPD coalition would not have had a majority in the national assembly. However, with 129 seats it would have become as large as the governing DJP.

By not including the NDRP it would also have been untainted by an authoritarian past. Toward the end of 1989 several newspaper reports predicted an imminent DJP-PPD coalition. This coalition was perceived by the journalists to be the result of the DJP's attempt to wash off its old image as an authoritarian governing party and of the PPD's attempt to portray itself as a moderate, rather than overly progressive, party (Kwon 1990). This coalition of the two larger parties would have produced a commanding majority in the national assembly.

Despite the puzzling make-up of the three-party coalition, the surprise merger in Korea has received scant attention in academia. According to Cotton, the merger was simply "the repetition of a political pattern" of prominent opposition leaders' taking turns in serving the interest of the governing party in Korea (Cotton 1992). Park maintains that the reason for the merger was "the commonality of interest between the three merged parties" (Park Jin 1990). Park's explanation is essentially correct, but he fails to specify the political actors' preferences in detail and thus cannot show why this particular coalition, out of the many possible coalitions, was formed.

The Assumption of Rationality and Coalition Theory

I assume that politicians are rational agents trying to maximize their self-interest. With the factors determining their interests (and thus their preferences) properly identified, we can explain why political actors choose certain courses of action. I further assume that, in the Korean context of coalition bargaining in 1990, party members' preferences coincided with their leaders' preferences. To the extent that this assumption is true, we can explain party behavior by looking at the interests of party leaders. The plausibility of this assumption is assessed in the final section of this chapter.

In this chapter, coalition theory is used to explain the party merger in Korea. Coalition theory is a branch of rational choice theory intended to explain the coalition behavior of different sets of rational actors. In political science it has been used to explain the formation of coalition governments in multiparty systems in Europe and elsewhere. Coalition theory dictates that two factors determine the coalition outcome: the relative power of the actors involved and their preferences over the important issues at hand. In the formation of coalition governments, the power of political parties is measured by the number of parliamentary seats they control, since the coalition needs to control a certain number of seats (the simple majority of parliamentary seats in most cases) to form a government. The important issue is usually social cleavage. In many countries, such as Sweden, a single cleavage divides parties along left-right ideological lines. Some countries, such as Spain and Belgium, have second or even third cleavages, along regional, ethnic-linguistic, and religious-secular lines. Actors' preferences on the important issues while forming coalition governments are reflected by the positions of political parties on these issues (cleavages). Coalition theory states simply that parties with similar preferences (issue positions) will form a coalition together. Therefore, in a country with a single left-right cleavage, a coalition of ideologically compatible parties is more likely than one composed of parties from the extreme right and left.

One may argue that coalition theory cannot explain mergers because merger and coalition are conceptually distinct phenomena. A coalition is a temporary union, while a merger is a permanent one. Given the simple logic of coalition theory, however, this difference should not pose a problem. Coalition theory states simply that each party's number of seats and preferences on important issues are most important in forming coalitions. As we shall see, the number of seats each party controlled at the time of the merger in Korea played a critical role in the formation of the DLP. Parties with similar preferences (positions on important issues) will join together whether they form a coalition government or merge their parties. Therefore, as long as we can correctly define the relevant issues (cleavages), coalition theory should adequately explain the party merger in Korea. I will use the term "coalition" in a broad sense to mean any type of collaboration among political parties, including merger.

Four Parties' Problems with the Four-Party System

The presidency of Roh Tae-woo, Chun Doo-hwan's successor, got off to a weak start when he won less than a majority in the 1987 presidential election. Even with a divided opposition, Roh received only 36.6 percent of the vote. In the thirteenth national assembly election, held in April 1988, the governing DJP won only 34 percent of the popular vote and only 125 seats, 25 fewer than the 150 needed for a majority. In comparison, the three opposition parties collectively held 164 seats (see table 3.1), the first time in

Table 3.1. Returns from the Thirteenth National Assembly Elections (April 1988).

Party	Number of Seats Won	Percentage of vote
Democratic Justice Party (DJP)	125 (129)*	34.0
New Democratic Republican Party (NDRP)	35	15.6
Reunification Democratic Party (RDP)	59	23.8
Party for Peace and Democracy (PPD)	70	19.3
Independents	10 (6)*	7.3
Total	299	100

Source: Cheng and Tallian (1992) and Brady and Mo (1992).
* Four national assemblymen elected as independents became members of the DJP by the latter half of 1989. Therefore, the DJP actually held 129 seats when the negotiation for the merger occurred.

Korean history the opposition held a majority of national assembly seats. Called *yeoso yadae* (small governing party–big opposition), the breakdown of seats in the assembly caused political deadlock, and the assembly failed to confirm the president's nominee for the chief justice of the Supreme Court. As early as summer 1988, leaders of the DJP began to call for a reorganization of the four-party system (*Dong-a Ilbo,* January 23, 1990).

The NDRP, the smallest of the four parties, could not assume power without first forming a coalition with another party (or parties). Kim Jong-pil, the leader of NDRP, was the first to call openly for reorganization of the existing political order in June 1988, only two months after the national assembly election (*Sisa Journal,* February 4, 1990).

The RDP had lost its status as the largest opposition party to the PPD in the national assembly elections and was often excluded from important legislative negotiations by the governing DJP and the PPD. The leaders of the RDP also had to worry about the decline of their party's base of support (Han Dong-yun 1990). For years the RDP had been perceived as a median party between the somewhat progressive PPD and the conservative (and authoritarian) DJP. The PPD drew its support from Cholla provinces and the urban disaffected, while the DJP was supported by the upper middle class, who wanted political stability. As the PPD became more moderate and the DJP's democratization program progressed, the RDP was squeezed in the middle. By June 1989, the RDP's Kim Young-sam was calling for "a new democracy," for a change in the existing system (*Sisa Journal,* February 4, 1990).

The PPD seemed to enjoy the new four-party system most among the four parties. As the largest opposition party, it negotiated directly with the governing DJP and sometimes excluded the rival RDP (Kim and Kim 1990). The PPD was drawn into the coalition game by the other three parties. Several members of the DJP (which had a regional origin in North Kyungsang province) called for a coalition with the PPD (with a regional origin in Cholla provinces) to overcome the decades-long regional cleavage in Korea. Several meetings took place among high-ranking officials of the two parties toward the end of 1989.[2]

Some sort of collaboration among the parties, if not merger, was forthcoming. However, which parties would form a coalition together? We first need to understand why the parties opted for merger instead of some sort of legislative collaboration that maintained separate party identities. More than a desire to break the legislative deadlock was at issue in the coalition bargaining of 1990. President Roh and the leaders of the DJP wanted to ensure their future security, for which they needed a supermajority governing party that could stay in power for a prolonged period of time. Under the presidential system in Korea, opposition parties do not participate in governing; small parties do not join the governing coalition as in multiparty parliamentary systems. Therefore, opposition parties in Korea are rarely rewarded for legislative collaboration with other parties. They can share political rewards (power) only by becoming a governing party. The more parties there are, the harder it is for any party to achieve this goal. To become a governing party, it is easier for it to merge with the existing governing party or to merge with other opposition parties and beat the governing party candidate in the next presidential election. The three Kims, the leaders of the three opposition parties, were known for their decades-long presidential aspirations, and they all knew these shortcuts to the presidency (Kim HeeMin 1992). In sum, the political interest of the leaders, of governing party and opposition alike, pointed to the merger of their parties rather than to legislative collaboration among them.

Determinants of Party Behavior

Korean parties were not constrained by the need to produce a coalition of a certain size since they were not forming a coalition government. However, political calculations determined the size of the coalition they preferred. The most important issue at the time of coalition bargaining in Korea was not social cleavage, as in most other countries, but rather leadership compatibility. Although other issues played a role in the coalition bargaining, leadership compatibility was the most important in shaping the course of events leading up to the party merger in 1990. Traditional social cleavages in Korea, such as ideological differences and regionalism, played only secondary roles in the merger.

The Size of the Coalition

Since Korea has a presidential system of government and such governments are not based on parliamentary majorities, the parties were not constrained by the requirement to produce a coalition of a certain size when they negotiated in 1989 and early 1990. Since a simple majority was not required, a coalition with fewer than half the seats in the national assembly was a possibility. A coalition of the NDRP and the RDP would have produced such a situation since these two parties combined had only 94 out of a total of 299 seats. Parties might want a simple majority coalition, since it would be able to pass most legislation, but not want to make the coalition too large, thereby reducing each party's share of rewards. A two-thirds majority is required for the national assembly to pass constitutional amendments. Therefore, parties with a desire for major systemic change would want a coalition that controlled at least two-thirds of the assembly's seats.

After the thirteenth national assembly election resulted in legislative deadlock, there was a discussion about whether the existing presidential system was desirable for Korea. Many politicians argued for a constitutional amendment that would allow a parliamentary system of government (Cheng and Tallian 1995). The merits and weaknesses of these two systems are not the immediate concern of this chapter. We can, however, make an intelligent conjecture about each party's preferred size of the future coalition based on the party's position on the constitutional amendment.

As early as summer 1988, leaders of the DJP called for a parliamentary system of government at the conclusion of Roh's term as president. It appears that they did so because President Roh and the leading members of the DJP were concerned about their future security.[3] They had been active participants in Chun Doo-hwan's coup in 1980 and the subsequent repression of opposition leaders. If the DJP lost power in a presidential election, some sort of political reprisal against them was foreseeable (Han Dong-yun 1990). This possibility was all too real after the dismal performance of Roh and the DJP in the 1987 presidential and 1988 national assembly elections. Moreover, the Korean constitution permits only one term for presidents, and the DJP had to find a replacement for Roh.

Intuitively, a parliamentary system government would have been safer for Roh and the leading members of the DJP, because it would have opened the door to the new governing party to prolong its rule. Under a parliamentary system the leader of the majority party (or coalition) becomes prime minister. As long as the new governing party maintained a majority, it would retain power. The DJP envisioned itself as the majority party in parliament. It appears to have been following the Japanese model, in which the Liberal Democratic Party held power for decades based on the majority of seats in the parliament.[4] Under this arrangement Roh would have been able to influence Korean politics even after his term as president. Since the DJP wanted a parliamentary system of government, which required a constitutional amendment, we can reasonably assume that the DJP's most preferred coalition size was one with a two-thirds majority of seats in the assembly.

By the time coalition bargaining began, Kim Jong-pil (NDRP) had repeatedly and publicly stated that the purpose of the negotiations was to build a stable parliamentary form of government (Kim and Kim 1990). It is not hard to imagine why leaders of the NDRP preferred a parliamentary system to the existing presidential system. The NDRP was the smallest party in the four-party system. Given the regional origins of the four parties and their leadership dynamics, it was not likely that the NDRP would ever lose its smallest party status—let alone assume power—under the existing system (Han Dong-yun 1990). Only under a parliamentary system would Kim Jong-pil and other leaders of the NDRP likely be considered candidates for prime minister or (the largely ceremonial) president sometime in the future as leaders of an important faction in the new party (Jang 1990). Since the creation of a parliamentary system required a constitutional amendment, we can assume that the NDRP also preferred a coalition that controlled at least two-thirds of the seats in the national assembly.

Kim Young-sam (RDP) shifted his "official" position on the type of constitutional government between the presidential and the parliamentary system over the years, while Kim Dae-jung (PPD) consistently supported the presidential system (Cheng and Tallian 1995). It is doubtful that Kim Young-sam ever seriously wanted a parliamentary system. He revealed his true preference for the presidential system after the new Democratic Liberal Party was formed. It is therefore questionable whether the two Kims, both of them supporters of the existing system, wanted a coalition with two-thirds of the national assembly seats as intensely as the leaders of the DJP and NDRP. They might have viewed such a majority as oversized. They probably preferred a bare majority coalition. With decades-long presidential ambitions, they had no reason to support a weak, submajority coalition as their first choice. In short, it is safe to say that all four parties' most preferred coalition size was at least a simple majority.

Leadership Compatibility

Parties' preferences on important political issues are also important in determining the outcome of coalition bargaining. The most important issue at the time of bargaining in Korea was leadership compatibility, rather than the traditional social cleavages of ideology and regionalism. Given future political interests of party leaders, which leaders would feel more comfortable belonging to the same coalition?

As I discussed in chapter 2, Kim Young-sam and Kim Dae-jung began to emerge as future leaders of the opposition at the 1970 national convention of the New Democratic Party, the major opposition party under Park Chung-hee's regime. Both Kims, relatively young men in their forties, argued for generational change in the party's leadership and sought its nomination for the scheduled presidential election of 1971 against the incumbent, President Park. Kim Dae-jung won the party's nomination for the presidency in the second ballot by a slim margin.[5]

As I also mentioned in chapter 2, the race for the nomination of the NDP in 1970 produced a strong rivalry between Kim Young-sam and Kim Dae-jung (Park Jin 1990). Since 1970 the two Kims have considered each other an eventual rival to overcome to become president if and when democracy is achieved in Korea. As such, they both tried to make sure their respective factions would be stronger with the opposition, while pursuing a democracy movement against the forces of Park Chung-hee and Chun Doo-hwan (Han Sung-joo 1990).

As I analyzed in chapter 2, the next encounter between the two Kims came at the time of the 1987 presidential election, the first direct presidential election in sixteen years. The two Kims failed to agree on a single presidential candidacy, and both of them ran for the presidency. As a result, Roh won the election with a plurality of only 36.6 percent of the votes, while Kim Young-sam and Kim Dae-jung received 28 and 27 percent, respectively.

Given their decades-long presidential ambitions, it was almost certain that both Kims would run for the president again in 1992. This time it was more likely that the winner of the contest between the two Kims would indeed emerge as the new president since no one in the governing DJP could match either Kim. Neither Kim wanted to form a coalition with the other and be forced to engage in an uncertain nomination battle when both could ensure nomination by their own parties. This political calculation of self-interest made the two Kims (and the RDP and PPD) least compatible at the time of coalition bargaining in 1990.

As for Kim Jong-pil, it was highly unlikely, given the relative weakness of the NDRP and leadership dynamics, that he would immediately emerge as a contender for the presidency. His long-term goal might have included the presidency (or the office of the prime minister if the constitution was changed). But the fact that he was not an immediate threat made him compatible to other leaders. Apparently, Kim Jong-pil himself chose Kim Young-sam as his political ally. Kim Jong-pil and Kim Young-sam, as well as other leaders of the NDRP and the RDP, held several meetings in 1989 at which they discussed the problem of the four-party system and "exchanged their evaluation of Kim Dae-jung's leadership and the PPD's policies." At one time or another, the possibility of a coalition of the NDRP and the RDP was raised in meetings between these two leaders (Han Dong-yun 1990). Kim Jong-pil and Kim Young-sam maintained a close political relationship. In contrast, Kim Jong-pil established no significant contact with Kim Dae-jung.

Interestingly, President Roh Tae-woo seemed to get along well with all three opposition leaders, despite the previous DJP regime's ostracization and imprisonment of them. He met individually with opposition leaders several times at the presidential residence for private discussions (Kim and Kim 1990). It appears that, as the leader of the governing DJP, he had much to offer these opposition leaders and was therefore attractive to them during the coalition bargaining. Opposition political leaders appeared to forego memories of the past (as what economists call a sunk cost) and acted as self-interest-maximizing political entrepreneurs in focusing on future political benefits.

Thus, Kim Young-sam and Kim Dae-jung were politically least compatible, Kim Jong-pil had close ties with Kim Young-sam, and Roh Taewoo was open to all three. If we assume that party members' preferences coincided with leaders' preferences, then leadership compatibility was identical to party compatibility in the coalition bargaining. According to the logic of coalition theory, parties with similar positions on an important issue dimension will form a coalition together. We therefore expect that parties close to one another on the issue of leadership compatibility would form a coalition together as long as leadership compatibility remained the most important issue during the coalition bargaining.

Analysis

All possible coalitions among the four parties are shown in figure 3.1. Each horizontal line represents a possible coalition containing the parties marked with black dots. The coalitions are numbered from the smallest number of seats to the largest.[6] As figure 3.1 shows, there were eleven possible coalitions from which the parties could choose. They included six two-party coalitions, four three-party coalitions, and a grand coalition of all four parties. A bare majority required 150 national assembly seats. Coalitions 4 through 7 are simple majority coalitions. A two-thirds majority required 200 seats. Coalitions 8 through 11 are two-thirds majority coalitions.

All parties preferred at least a bare majority. No party preferred a submajority coalition. If the parties tried to form a coalition of their preferred size, then we can safely exclude submajority coalitions 1 through 3 from consideration, leaving eight possible coalitions with at least a bare majority of seats in the assembly.

Of the eight remaining coalitions, three contain both the RDP and PPD, the parties of Kim Young-sam and Kim Dae-jung, respectively. Because of leadership rivalry, the RDP and the PPD would not have agreed to form a coalition together unless their refusal totally excluded them from any new coalition. Thus, we may safely rule out those coalitions containing both the RDP and the PPD (4, 10, 11) from further consideration.

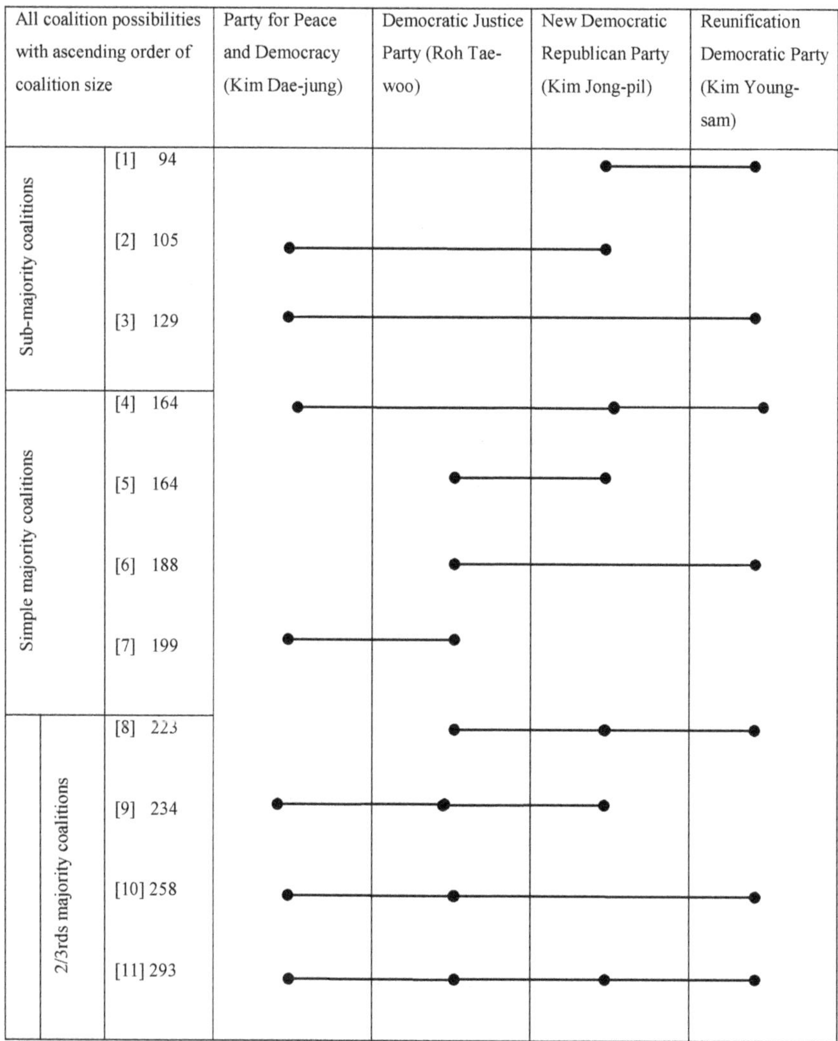

All coalition possibilities with ascending order of coalition size
Party for Peace and Democracy (Kim Dae-jung)
Democratic Justice Party (Roh Tae-woo)
New Democratic Republican Party (Kim Jong-pil)
Reunification Democratic Party (Kim Young-sam)
Sub-majority coalitions
[1] 94
[2] 105
[3] 129
Simple majority coalitions
[4] 164
[5] 164
[6] 188
[7] 199
2/3rds majority coalitions
[8] 223
[9] 234
[10] 258
[11] 293

Fig. 3.1 Coalition possibilities at the time of coalition bargaining among Korean political parties.

A close look at the remaining coalitions (5 through 9) reveals a shocking fact: the governing DJP is in all five of them! The DJP was what social choice theorists call a "veto player." Without it, a winning coalition could not be formed. The governing DJP was practically in a position to choose its coalition partner(s)—that is, to choose one out of the five feasible coalitions. The DJP wanted a constitutional amendment to allow a parliamentary system of government and thus preferred a coalition with two-thirds of the national assembly seats. Among the five feasible coalitions, those with a two-thirds majority were most likely to be chosen by the DJP. Coalitions 8 and 9 fit this criterion.

Between DJP-NDRP-RDP and PPD-DJP-NDRP coalitions, the former was more compatible in terms of leadership. On January 22, 1990, at the Blue House, the presidential residence, Roh Tae-woo, Kim Jong-pil, and Kim Young-sam proclaimed the merger of the DJP, NDRP, and RDP and the birth of the new Democratic Liberal Party.

Discussion

The DJP seems to have gotten its best possible outcome out of all possible coalitions, the DJP-NDRP-RDP merger. The new party now controlled more than the two-thirds majority necessary to change the constitution so that a parliamentary system could become the new form of government in Korea. Leaders were also compatible with one another in this coalition. The new Democratic Liberal Party appeared to have been the best possible outcome for the NDRP as well, because it also wanted a parliamentary system of government. Can we say the same for the RDP? The RDP was not as supportive of constitutional change as the DJP and NDRP. If we drop from all possible coalitions those without the RDP in them (the RDP's least preferred coalitions) and those containing both RDP and PPD (only slightly more preferable), we are left with three possibilities. A coalition between the NRPD and RDP was precarious because it left room for a coalition between the DJP and PPD, the two largest parties, which were also the governing party and the party of Kim Dae-jung, Kim Young-sam's major political rival. Thus, the merger of January 1990 was one of the two best possible outcomes for the RDP as well. Moreover, since three of the parties were getting their best possible outcomes, the PPD could offer little, had no room for negotiation, and thus was excluded.

All feasible coalitions included the DJP, making it a veto player. However, the DJP did not seem to realize that the new Democratic Liberal Party was a minimal winning coalition if the decision rule was two-thirds rule. The departure of any one party from the coalition made it non-winning, because it then failed to maintain two-thirds of the seats in the national assembly and a constitutional amendment became impossible (Riker 1962). Theoretically, although the DJP was the veto player in *the coalition formation game,* now every party (every faction in the new party to be exact) became a veto player in *a coalition maintenance game.* Every party was on an equal footing regardless of its size. Kim Young-sam and the RDP never really wanted a parliamentary system. Only months after the formation of the Democratic Liberal Party, Kim Young-sam successfully silenced calls for a constitutional amendment by threatening to leave the new party with his faction, the old RDP (Han Dong-yun 1990; Jang 1990). The existing presidential system was maintained. In 1992 Kim Young-sam became the presidential nominee of the Democratic Liberal Party, and in December 1992 he was elected president, defeating the opposition candidate, Kim Dae-jung.

The coalition of the DJP, NDRP, and RDP was nevertheless puzzling because these parties had very different roots. Each party's preferred size for the new coalition and the issue of leadership compatibility played the decisive roles in creating this coalition, rather than left-right ideological and regional cleavages. Party positions (preferences) on size and compatibility were the positions of party leaders and were determined by the leaders' political interest. We can conclude that party leaders pursued their own interests in the coalition bargaining. Can we say the same for the followers? Followers are defined as the incumbent national assemblymen for each party, since the leaders were counting the number of national assembly seats in their coalition bargaining. I have assumed that the party members' (followers') preferences coincided with their leaders' preferences and that the self-interests of national assemblymen coincided with their leaders' interests. Certain features of Korean politics make this assumption plausible.

First, for decades Korean politics has been dominated by a few individuals, such as Park Chung-hee, Kim Jong-pil, Chun Doo-hwan, Roh Tae-woo, Kim Young-sam, and Kim Dae-jung. Most individual members of the national assembly owed their rise to power to one of these leaders (Han Myung-kyu 1990). The dominance of a few leaders bred paternalistic political parties. Followers give their loyalty to one dominant leader, and in return the leader takes care of his followers by helping them with campaign finances and making sure loyal followers are nominated in their districts (Han Myung-kyu 1990). Therefore, the followers' welfare tends to be maximized when the leaders' wishes are realized—that is, when the leader has greater ability to deliver political benefits. At the time of the party merger in Korea, the political parties had exactly this kind of paternalistic nature. President Roh in the DJP, Kim Jong-pil in the NDRP, Kim Young-sam in the RDP, and Kim Dae-jung in the PPD were the dominant leaders.

Second, Korean political parties traditionally have not contested the candidacy for national assembly seats within districts. Rather, candidates are nominated by party leaders. Leaders can single-handedly deny an incumbent assemblyman the candidacy in the next election if they so choose (Sohn 1989). Thus, national assemblymen's reelection and ultimately their careers rest in the hands of a few party leaders. Interestingly, Kim Young-sam and Kim Dae-jung, who had fought for decades for the democratization of the country, maintained an extremely authoritarian system of candidate selection within their own parties.

The paternalistic nature of Korean parties and the authoritarian nomination system made followers totally dependent on party leaders for political survival. They lacked the ability to stand on their own without the leaders' help (Han Myung-kyu 1990). At the time of the coalition bargaining in Korea, followers had a choice between going along with the merger, designed to maximize their leaders' interests, and opposing it and not joining the new party if it materialized. Given party members' total dependence on their leaders, it was highly unlikely they would survive politically if the merger were realized and they were left out of it (Jang 1990). To the extent that politicians are motivated by office and power, it was in the interests of these followers to support the proposed merger and then try to build their power within the framework of the proposed DLP. How many followers from the DJP, NDRP, and RDP accepted the merger that seemed to benefit their leaders?

Shortly before the party merger, one DJP assemblyman died, and another resigned for his role in the bloody crackdown of a citizen uprising a decade earlier. Thus, there were 221 potential members of the DLP, including 127 DJP, 35 NDRP, and 59 RDP assemblypersons, of whom 215 joined the new DLP. This pattern of behavior clearly shows that leaders and followers alike pursued their self-interest in the coalition bargaining and three-party merger in 1990.[7]

Postscript

In 1995, following a revelation by an opposition assemblyman, former president Roh Tae-woo was arrested for illegally receiving bribes from business conglomerates and accumulating slush funds during his term as president. By the time Roh's trial began in December 1995, investigators uncovered more than $600 million in illegally obtained funds. With skyrocketing public anger, two former presidents, Roh and Chun Doo-hwan, were also indicted in January 1996 for mutiny and sedition in connection with their roles in the military coup and bloody crackdown on civilian demonstrators in 1980. On February 6, 1996, the Democratic Liberal Party formally changed its name to the New Korea Party (NKP) to create a fresh image (but with the same people). At this point, it appeared that the personal security of President Roh and other former leading members of the DJP was uncertain. Since the major motivation of the DJP leaders in merging with the RDP and NDRP had been their future security, they had failed to achieve their goal despite the party merger. The critical point came when Kim Young-sam refused to go along with the constitutional amendment for a parliamentary system of government. Nevertheless, Roh's failure does not make him irrational (or less rational) and does not weaken rational choice theory. Rational choice theory does not presume that actors possess perfect and complete knowledge about future events. It merely assumes that, given the information they have, they try to pursue the best available means to achieve their end. With the information he had before the merger about parties' preferences and available means, Roh Tae-woo chose what he believed would best achieve his goal, the guarantee of personal security. He could not foresee Kim Young-sam's defection after the merger, and this should not make Roh Tae-woo retrospectively appear irrational.

4

A Theory of Government-Driven Democratization

The Kim Young-sam Years

The thirteenth National Assembly election in Korea in 1988, a democratic one, created a four-party system. Within two years, in January 1990, the Democratic Liberal Party was formed as a grand conservative coalition through a merger of three existing parties: the governing Democratic Justice Party (DJP) with military connections; the New Democratic Republican Party (NDRP) led by Kim Jong-pil, an ex-prime minister under the Park Chung-hee regime; and the Reunification Democratic Party (RDP) led by a long-time member of the opposition, Kim Young-sam. The birth of the Democratic Liberal Party put an end to the four-party system and effectively replaced it with a two-party system. Excluded from the coalition was the Party for Peace and Democracy (PPD), led by another long-time opposition leader, Kim Dae-jung.

The coalition of the DJP, NDRP, and RDP is puzzling since these parties do not seem to have much in common. The NDRP was the successor party to the Democratic Republican Party, the authoritarian governing party under Park Chung-hee (1961–1979). The RDP was the successor party to the New Democratic Party, the opposition party to Park's rule. The governing DJP was founded by Chun Doo-hwan after his successful military coup in 1980. When he took power, Chun disbanded all of the political parties of the previous regime and banned the political activities of all the major political figures, including Kim Jong-pil, Kim Young-sam, and Kim Dae-jung, with charges against them ranging from financial wrongdoings to inciting riots. It was not until 1987 that all three Kims were allowed to resume their political activities. In short, all three Kims suffered from Chun's rule. The leaders of the RDP had said all along that the DJP should not have been born in the first place.

The study of the party merger is interesting, given the rush to democratization occurring throughout the world. Born out of the collapse of the old system, most of these new would-be democracies in Eastern Europe, Latin America, and Asia are under pressure to rebuild their economies while maintaining stable political systems. These tasks require strong government. The Korean example is interesting in that at the time the party merger occurred: (1) the country's democratization program had continued since 1987; (2) the country's once miraculous economy had slowed down after democratization began (although the causes of the slowdown may not have been entirely political); and (3) the legislative processes were deadlocked due to the weak presidency and the minority governing party. What emerged out of the merger in 1990 was a seemingly stable and strong supermajority governing party.

I have shown in the previous chapter that the coalition of DJP, NDRP, and RDP was driven mainly by the political interests of the actors and parties involved rather than an attempt to break the legislative deadlock. Nevertheless, the Korean public did not punish the parties for the merger in the national assembly and presidential elections in 1992. In this chapter, I will discuss the implications of the merger and the two elections of 1992 for the democratization process in Korea. Mainly, I argue that in a country like Korea, the democratization process, once started, is likely to be driven by the government due to the country's unusual past economic development.

The 1990 Conservative Coalition

After months of behind-closed-doors negotiations, on January 22, 1990, Roh Tae-woo, Kim Jong-pil, and Kim Young-sam proclaimed the merger of the DJP, NDRP, and RDP and the birth of the new Democratic Liberal Party (DLP). It controlled over two-thirds of the seats in the national assembly. The DLP contained the RDP (Kim Young-sam's party) but not the PPD (Kim Dae-jung's party), and thus was compatible leadership-wise. It was also ideologically connected (Axelrod 1970), and more coherent in terms of the regional origins of the member parties, although I do not believe regionalism was a serious factor in the coalition bargaining.

The DJP seemed to have the best possible outcome, namely the DJP-NDRP-RDP merger, where the new party now controlled 215 seats, fifteen more than the two-thirds majority necessary to change the constitution so that a parliamentary system could become the new form of government in Korea.[1] This new party seemed to be ideologically coherent in the sense that the three least progressive parties merged themselves into one. For exactly the same reason, the new Democratic Liberal Party was the best possible outcome for the NDRP as well, which also wanted a parliamentary system of government. Can we say the same for the RDP? We need to remember that the RDP may not have been as supportive of the constitutional change as the DJP and the NDRP.

As I mentioned in the previous chapter, there were only three possible coalitions that the RDP would like to see form, since all other possible coalitions either did not include the RDP (which must have been the RDP's least preferred coalitions) or included both the RDP and the PPD (which were probably only slightly preferable to the first group of coalitions). These three coalitions were DJP-RDP, NDRP-RDP, and DJP-NDRP-RDP. The second coalition, NDRP-RDP, was a precarious possibility since it left room for the DJP-PPD coalition, the coalition of the two largest parties, and also the coalition of the governing party and the party of Kim Dae-jung, Kim Young-sam's major political rival. We can say that what actually formed in January of 1990 was one of the two best possible outcomes for the RDP as well.

Post-Merger Maneuvering

We need to note that the DJP-NDRP-RDP coalition was what Riker calls a minimal winning coalition *if the decision rule is a two-thirds majority.* That is, the departure of any one party from the coalition makes it a nonwinning coalition (Riker 1962). If *any* one party leaves the coalition, it fails to maintain two-thirds of the seats in the national assembly, and constitutional amendment becomes impossible. Therefore, every party was on an equal footing regardless of its size. It is not hard to guess who was the first to defect after the coalition was formed. As we recall, Kim Young-sam and the RDP never really wanted the parliamentary system in the first place. Only months after the formation of the Democratic Liberal Party, Kim Young-sam successfully silenced the call for a constitutional amendment by threatening to leave the party with his faction (that is, the old RDP). The existing presidential system was maintained. In 1992, Kim Young-sam, after a period of intense struggle within the party, became the presidential nominee for the Democratic Liberal Party.

One may ask why the old DJP and NDRP factions in the DLP did not break with the RDP once it became apparent that the parliamentary system was impossible due to Kim Young-sam's defection. There are many explanations for this. First, the political atmosphere had changed by this time. The old DJP did not act as a single entity anymore; instead, the old DJP had been split into at least three different factions, with distinct "middle bosses" (see Beck 1993 and Park 1990 for the factionalism within the DLP). Second, the way politicians sold the merger to the public restricted their options. They presented the merger as "an attempt to bury past conflicts, heal past wounds," and as "a decision to save the nation" (*Dong-a Ilbo,* January 23, 1990). If the new governing party had broken up within months of its establishment, the breakup would not only have been embarrassing to incumbent President Roh, but might have eroded his power and effectiveness as president for the remainder of his term (Park Jin 1990). Third, President Roh, who was concerned about his future security, had to be prepared for a couple of alternative scenarios: one in which Kim Young-sam emerged as the standard-bearer of the DLP in 1992, and another in which Kim Young-sam, in desperation, left the DLP along with his old RDP, gave up his own political ambition, and supported Kim Dae-jung's presidency in 1992. The latter scenario was especially threatening to Roh, given the facts that the two Kims collectively outvoted Roh with 55 to 36.6 percent of the total votes cast in 1987 and that there was no one in the DLP who could match either Kim's political stature. In sum, due to unforeseen changes in the political atmosphere, the DJP became vulnerable to the RDP's threat after the coalition was formed.

Shortly after the merger of three parties in 1990, the PPD, which was excluded from the merger, absorbed five former members of the RDP who did not join the DLP (see note 4.1) and two independents, and changed its name to the Democratic Party (DP). With the fourteenth national assembly election approaching, a new Unification National Party (UNP) was founded by Chung Ju-yong, chairman of the Hyundai Corporation, one of the largest business conglomerates in Korea.

The Elections of 1992

Both the national assembly elections and the presidential election were scheduled in 1992. It would be the first time that Korean citizens had a chance to punish or reward the governing DLP for the 1990 merger. This was so not only because elections are the most common channel through which the public rewards or punishes politicians and parties for their past behavior in a representative political system, but also because the merger continued to be a major political issue. Ever since the merger, the PPD had referred to it as "a coup d'état against democracy" (Lee 1990, 132) and to Kim Young-sam as a traitor to the opposition and an opportunist not to be trusted (Han Dong-yun 1990). Naturally, the merger became a campaign issue and the media participated in creating the political atmosphere of a judgment day.

The fourteenth national assembly election was held in March 1992. The DLP won 149 seats, one seat shy of the simple majority. That is, the governing DLP, with over two-thirds of the seats in the previous assembly, turned into a submajority party. The Democratic Party increased its seats to ninety-seven, while the splinter Unification National Party shocked observers by securing thirty-one seats. What was also unique about the fourteenth national assembly election was the record twenty-one independents who were elected (see table 4.1). The election results were described by the media as a stunning defeat for the governing DLP and as punishment for ignoring the people's will by merging parties without their approval (see *The Economist*, March 28, 1992, and *Hankuk Ilbo*, March 26, 1992, among others).

The presidential election followed the national assembly election in December. Seven candidates were running, but four represented obscure parties, so they did not have a realistic chance of winning the election. The race was essentially among three candidates: Kim Young-sam, representing the governing DLP; Kim Dae-jung of the Democratic Party;

Table 4.1. Returns from the Fourteenth National Assembly Elections (March 1992).

Party	Number of seats won	Percentage of vote
Democratic Liberal Party	149	38.5
Democratic Party	97	29.2
Unification National Party	31	17.4
Others*	22	14.9
Total	299	100

Source: Hankuk Ilbo, March 26, 1992.
* This total includes 21 independents and one assemblyman from an obscure party.

Table 4.2. Returns from the 1992 Presidential Election (December 1992).

Candidate	Number of votes won	Percentage of vote
Kim Young-sam (DLP)	9,977,322	41.4
Kim Dae-jung (DP)	8,041,284	33.4
Chung Ju-yong (UNP)	3,880,067	16.1
Others*	2,196,170	9.1
Total	24,094,843	100

Source: Dong-a Ilbo, December 19, 1992.
* There were four candidates representing obscure parties.

and billionaire-turned-politician Chung Ju-yong. The race was considered to be tight especially because Chung Ju-yong was appealing to those who did not want to vote for either Kim, sort of a Korean version of the Ross Perot phenomenon. According to Chung, the difference between Perot and himself was that he (Chung Ju-yong) had more money and he also had his own party. The actual election result was a rather easy victory for the governing party candidate, Kim Young-sam, largely due to Chung Ju-yong's below-expectation performance (also similar to Perot). Kim Young-sam received 41.4 percent of the total votes cast, beating Kim Dae-jung by nearly 2 million votes.

The Lack of Citizen Punishment

In this section, I evaluate how severe citizen punishment actually was for the 1990 merger with the returns from the two elections reported earlier. I argue that although the DLP lost many seats, becoming a submajority party, and the opposition DP gained about twenty seats, the Korean public still did not punish the governing DLP as harshly as the numbers seem to suggest.

First, at the time of the thirteenth national assembly election in 1987, there were three opposition parties and the governing DJP, so opposition candidates had to spilt opposition votes while the DJP candidate more or less monopolized governing party/conservative votes. By the fourteenth national assembly election, an unexpected difficulty arose for the DLP as the new Unification National Party, being founded by a billionaire, was viewed as ideologically closer to the governing DLP than the opposition

DP. Now that the DP candidates in each district were sweeping opposition votes and the DLP candidate had to fight the UNP for governing party/conservative votes, it was not surprising to see the DP increase its seats by about twenty.

Second, out of twenty-one independents elected, nineteen had ties to the governing party: One of them was a former RDP assemblyman; fifteen had sought the DLP's nomination as members of the DJP faction, had run as independents when they failed to get nomination, and had been elected; the remaining three were former DJP assemblymen. Sooner or later, most of them joined the governing DLP (*Hankuk Ilbo*, March 26, 1992).

Third, ninety-two incumbents failed to get reelected in the fourteenth national assembly election, a rather large number given the size of the national assembly with 299 seats. If we look at the partisanship of these ninety-two, however, sixty-three were governing DLP members and the remaining twenty-nine were non-DLP members (*Hankuk Ilbo*, March 26, 1992). Given the fact that over two-thirds of all the incumbents were DLP assemblymen before the election, the proportion of the defeated DLP incumbents (63/92) was about the same as the proportion of the seats held by the DLP in the previous national assembly (217/299). The point is that the Korean people did not seem to single out DLP incumbents to punish them.

Then, despite the DLP's loss of many seats in the national assembly, we can say that it was not particularly harshly punished by the public for the 1990 merger. The DLP easily went over the simple majority of seats by absorbing many independents after the election, and as the UNP crumbled following Chung Ju-yong's poor performance in the presidential election, it absorbed several UNP assemblymen as well.

Now to the presidential election. It was generally expected that Chung Ju-yong would steal enough moderate to conservative and upper-middle class voters from Kim Young-sam and that Kim Dae-jung should be able to hold on to the two southwestern provinces and the urban disaffected. These factors would make the race among the three anybody's pick. Although Kim Dae-jung held on to his traditional supporters, Chung's expected sprint toward election day did not happen, and the result was Kim Young-sam's (unexpectedly) convincing win with 41.4 percent of the total votes cast. Out of fifteen provinces and specially administered municipalities in Korea, Kim Young-sam came in first in all but three.

These three were Kim Dae-jung's strongholds: the two southwestern provinces and the capital city of Seoul. Even in Seoul, Kim Young-sam almost upset Kim Dae-jung by receiving 36.3 percent of the votes, compared to Kim Dae-jung's 37.7 percent. Out of forty-four districts in Seoul, Kim Young-sam actually outvoted Kim Dae-jung in fifteen (*Dong-a Ilbo*, December 19, 1992). Most of these were upper-middle class residential districts south of the Han River. Certainly Kim Young-sam did not seem to be punished for the 1990 merger or for "betraying the opposition."

Government-Driven Democratization

Although the whole party system change was brought about to meet the political interests of the politicians, they were not severely punished by the people, as we saw in the election results above. This was the case because by 1990 the general mood of the country demanded political and economic stability after two years of economic slowdown and political deadlock (see table 4.3).

Therefore, the 1990 merger was a fairly low-risk merger. The expected cost of the merger was particularly low because Koreans had become used to a high rate of economic growth, which made them intolerant of instability (see table 4.4). Any economic performance, say, below the annual growth rate of 6 percent means an economic crisis. Therefore, the stable

Table 4.3. Economic Slowdown, 1987–1989.

Indicator	1987	1988	1989
GNP growth rate	12%	–	6.7%
Growth rate in manufacturing	18.8%	13.4%	3.7%
Export growth rate	36.2%	28.4%	2.6%

Source: Facts about Korea, Korean Overseas Information Service, 1991.
Note: Average annual inflation rate, 1984–1987: 2.5%. Inflation rate, 1990 (first three quarters): 9%.

Table 4.4. Economic Development, 1962–1990.

Indicator	1962	1975	1990
Gross National Product*	$2.3	$20.8	$237.9
Per capita GNP	$87	$590	$5,569
Domestic savings rate	3.3%	–	37.7%

Source: Facts about Korea, Korean Overseas Information Service, 1991.
* In billions of dollars (current price = 1985).

political system that the merger seemed to deliver was a public good for many Koreans. In this way, the parties' interest in the merger coincided with the citizen demand for stability.

A solid core of middle-class citizens, produced by the attainment of a certain level of economic development, demanded democracy in 1987, which at least partially explains the introduction of democratic measures in Korea (Cheng and Krause 1991; Cotton 1992; Han Sung-joo 1990; Kihl 1988; and Moon 1988). The very middle class, however, also supports stability. As long as the government's democratization program satisfies their basic expectations, they will continue to support a stable system based on strong (but democratic) government. That is why I believe that the process of democratization in Korea will be essentially government driven: the political elites will initiate democratic measures, and the middle class will respond by continuing to support the governing party in elections. In a similar vein, Cheng (1990) argues that the middle class in Korea was the last one to join the anti-authoritarian social coalition, but the first one to defect from it once democratization was in order.

Here we need to note that between the two public goods of economic growth and political stability, Koreans value the former much more than the latter, per se. The whole premise of the Korean electorate's preference for strong government was its belief that the stable political systems would produce the continued economic growth that Koreans were used to. So, the real point was about a strong economy rather than a stable system. And back in the early to mid-1990s, Koreans (including myself) believed that the latter would deliver the former.

The Asian financial crisis of 1997, however, hit the Korean economy extremely hard following three decades of remarkable economic growth. The South Korean economy fell prey to a sudden collapse in November 1997, alarming the entire world. After a series of financial and foreign exchange crises, the Kim Young-sam government filed for national economic bankruptcy by asking the International Monetary Fund (IMF) for $57 billion in bail-out funds in December 1997. The myth of the South Korean economic miracle was shattered.

During Kim Young-sam's term in office, South Korea's foreign debts increased from $43.9 billion to $160.7 billion in 1996, while foreign reserve assets dwindled from $20.2 billion in 1993 to $12.4 billion in 1997. At the peak of the currency crisis, foreign reserves held by the central bank were less than $8 billion, spreading the fear of default. With foreign reserves being depleted, the Korean currency rapidly depreciated. Korean currency dropped to nearly half its value against the American dollar by December, 1997.

More troublesome was the private sector. The banking and financial sector as well as the corporate sector showed their worst performance in recent history. Economic output dropped more than 10 percent in six months. The economy plunged 6.7 percent in 1998. The large debts caused the corporate sectors to draw back investments and make large cuts in employment and wages. The unemployment rate quadrupled to 8 percent by the end of 1998, and domestic spending was reduced. The average annual stock price index was 808.1 in 1993 and 1,027.4 in 1994. But it continued a downward slide throughout 1995 and 1996, falling to 375 by the end of 1997, its lowest level since the opening of the securities markets. The reason for Korea's high vulnerability to the crisis is thought to have been the corporate sector's high level of debt, a weakened financial system from corporate bankruptcies in early 1997, and the fact that Korea's short-term foreign debt was high compared to its international reserves.

Although Korea's economic crisis was caused mainly by the long-term economic structural problems, it happened during the latter half of Kim Young-sam's term. His government was supposed to deliver a stable political system, which many Koreans believed was the sufficient condition for fast economic growth, after the three-party merger. As I mentioned above, Korean people's real concern was economic growth rather than strong government, and it reacted to the total failure of the Kim Young-sam government.

In July 1997, a former supreme court judge and prime minister, Lee Hoi-chang, was nominated as presidential candidate for the governing NKP for the upcoming presidential election. In September, Governor Rhee In-je of Kyonggi Province announced that he would secede from the ruling party to run in the December presidential election on the ticket of a new party he would establish. On October 28, the National Congress for New Politics (NCNP) and the United Liberal Democrats (ULD) agreed to field NCNP leader Kim Dae-jung as their joint presidential candidate and to revise the state constitution by the end of 1999 to introduce a parliamentary system of government, under which the ULD's Kim Jong-pil would become prime minister. In November, Rhee In-je was chosen the presidential candidate of the New Party by the People (NPP), which he organized with the help of defectors from the governing party. On November 21, the governing NKP merged itself with a minor party, the Democratic Party (DP), and changed its name to the Grand National Party (GNP).

In the presidential election held on December 18, 1997, the joint opposition candidate, Kim Dae-jung, received 40.3 percent of the total votes cast; Lee Hoi-chang received 38.7 percent; and Rhee In-je received 19.2 percent. The 1.6 percent difference between Kim Dae-jung and Lee Hoi-chang amounts to only 390,000 votes out of over 26 million. So, Kim Dae-jung finally got elected the president of Korea in his fourth attempt.

It is safe to say that the economic crisis, coupled with the pre-election coalition of the two largest opposition parties and an independent candidacy of the former governing party member, led to the first peaceful transfer of political power in fifty years. The Kim Dae-jung government, which was inaugurated in February 1998, implemented IMF conditionalities methodically. Most structural adjustment measures, such as banking and financial reform, reform of big business, and labor reform, all of which were conceived of as early as the 1980s, but were delayed for political reasons, were implemented within one year of his reign. And the South Korean economy began to demonstrate a remarkable pace of recovery.

Given the rush to democratization occurring throughout the world, and the fact that most of these countries have the double task of rebuilding their economies and maintaining stable political systems, the cost of stability-inducing political measures (such as the level of citizen punishment in an election), whatever the motivation, is likely to be low in most of these countries as long as they are not viewed as a reversion to authoritarianism. The extent to which the Korean experience provides a model for the new democracies is yet to be seen.

5

Party Preferences and Institutional Choices

A Search for a New Electoral System

The relationships between electoral systems, parties, and election outcomes have long been studied in political science. There have been theoretical studies of these relationships (see, for example, Duverger 1951; Riker 1982; Palfrey 1989) as well as empirical research (see Rae 1967; Taagepera and Shugart 1989; Lijphart 1990). These relationships have received renewed attention, since many countries in Eastern Europe and elsewhere have been searching for new forms of electoral institutions at a time of democratic transition from previously authoritarian rule (for example, Brady and Mo 1992; Lijphart 1994; Cheng and Tallian 1995; Cox 1997; Sartori 1997; Kostadinova 1999).

It is generally assumed in studies of institutions and democratic transitions that political actors are capable of foreseeing the impact of alternative electoral institutions at the time they bargain for new forms of institutions. Therefore, they try to install an electoral system that will satisfy their various political objectives.

Korea in 1998 (and beyond) presents an interesting case. The democratically elected government of Kim Dae-jung had the task of reviving the national economy from its unprecedented economic crisis. When Kim Dae-jung's government came to power, it promised to implement political reform (that is, to devise new political institutions), including a new set of electoral institutions. As rational actors, the members of the Kim government would try to see to it that the new political institutions would promote their own political objectives and those of their party, the National Conference for New Politics (NCNP). The questions were (1) whether a set of institutions could satisfy political actors' various objectives simultaneously, and (2) how would these politicians react in the absence of such a set of institutions? This chapter tries to answer these questions.

In the next two sections of this chapter, I review officially stated as well as unstated objectives of the NCNP's political reform and introduce alternative electoral institutions proposed by various political actors. After attempting to predict the consequences of various electoral institutions by utilizing the statistics of the 1996 national assembly elections and the 1998 local government elections, I assess whether these electoral institutions could achieve the NCNP's objectives introduced earlier. I conclude the chapter by offering an explanation of why the governing NCNP stressed the need for the so-called *political reorganization* in addition to political reform.

The Objectives of Political Reform

Long-time opposition leader Kim Dae-jung came to power through a direct presidential election in December 1997. Upon assuming power, the Kim government began pushing for the restructuring of the economy, including reforms in management and labor practices as well as administrative reform. As time passed, the Kim government came under increasing pressure for political reform as well, since the public demanded that politicians share the burden of the restructuring effort sweeping the country. Under these conditions, the Kim government and the governing NCNP in 1998 proposed a series of political reforms, including reforms in electoral system, party system, and the national assembly, and promised a greater level of local autonomy (*Joongang Ilbo,* February 28, June 23, July 2, August 15, 1998).

According to President Kim Dae-jung and the leaders of the NCNP, the objectives of this political reform included (1) lower costs for elections; (2) accurate reflection of public opinion through a new electoral system (*Joongang Ilbo,* March 3, 1998); and (3) the transformation of the NCNP from a regional party to a party with nationwide support (*Joongang Ilbo,* June 18, 1998). The NCNP also began to emphasize (4) the need for the governing coalition (the NCNP and the ULD) to control a stable majority of the national assembly seats (*Joongang Ilbo,* September 5, 1998). Besides these "officially stated" objectives, Korea specialists generally agree that there was another important objective of the political reform: (5) preventing any single opposition party from blocking a potential constitutional amendment, *or* enabling the NCNP to block any future attempts at constitutional amendment.

To see why these objectives are important, we need to understand historical events leading up to Kim Dae-jung's election as president. Then-opposition NCNP candidate Kim Dae-jung was able to defeat the governing and majority Grand National Party (GNP) candidate Lee Hoi-chang in the presidential election in December 1997. His victory was not necessarily due to his party's popularity but rather was based on his personal charisma and popularity and the coalition with Kim Jong-pil and the United Liberal Democrats (ULD). From the day he was sworn in as the new president, Kim Dae-jung had to face a majority opposition party, the GNP. As expected, the GNP became extremely antagonistic toward, and uncooperative with, the Kim administration and the NCNP within the national assembly. Most of the Kim government's reform initiatives were put on hold by the majority GNP in the national assembly. It took almost half a year for Kim Jong-pil, President Kim's prime minister designee, to get the required ratification of the national assembly—he had to serve as an acting prime minister during the first five months of the Kim government. Given this background and with an urgent need to concentrate on reviving the national economy, President Kim and the governing coalition members began to express the need to build a political system in which the NCNP-ULD coalition controlled a stable majority within the national assembly.[1]

President Kim Dae-jung and Kim Jong-pil, the leader of the ULD, had very different political roots. Kim Dae-jung was a prominent opposition figure and champion of democracy during the Park Chung-hee regime (1961–1979), while Kim Jong-pil was a core member of General Park's successful coup d'état group in 1961 and a prime minister under Park. Ideologically, the former represented a liberal cause throughout his political career while the latter represented a bastion of conservatism in Korean political circles. As different as they were, these experienced politicians also understood that neither of them was likely to be elected president with their and their parties' regional support bases. Under this background, they got together and formed a coalition of their parties just before the presidential election in 1997. The goal of this coalition was for Kim Dae-jung to be elected president of the country. Given the narrow margin of his victory over Lee Hoi-chang (representing the GNP), fewer than 400,000 votes out of over 26 million votes cast, the coalition between the two parties was critical for Kim Dae-jung's victory in 1997.

Of course, Kim Jong-pil's and the ULD's support of Kim Dae-jung's candidacy was not a freebie. Both leaders and their parties openly agreed before the election that Kim Jong-pil would be named prime minister if Kim Dae-jung was elected, and that there would be a constitutional amendment, before Kim Dae-jung's term ended, changing the country's political system from a presidential system to a parliamentary system. It is widely known that Kim Jong-pil has been a longtime advocate of South Korea's adopting a parliamentary system.

Given the agreement between the NCNP and the ULD on the constitutional amendment, they would not want some other party to control enough votes within the national assembly to be able to block its passage. Under Korean law, two-thirds of the votes in the national assembly are required for a constitutional amendment. This means that there should be no party outside of the NCNP and the ULD coalition with more than one-third of the seats in the national assembly. The Korean national assembly has 299 seats, and one-third of the seats is 100. At the time Kim Dae-jung came in as president, the GNP controlled 161 seats. This meant that the governing coalition would have to come up with a political reform measure that could ensure that the GNP would lose seats.

The argument above is true *if Kim Dae-jung and the NCNP intended to honor the agreement with Kim Jong-pil and the ULD.* There was some chance that the former might not keep their word about the constitutional amendment to change the political system. Kim Dae-jung had believed in the presidential form of government throughout his political career, as seen in the previous chapters. He apparently agreed to a constitutional change in an attempt to acquire Kim Jong-pil's support in the presidential election. The president had a perfect excuse for not keeping his word, mainly the financial crisis the country was undergoing and an apparent need to maintain political stability to overcome economic difficulties. It could easily be argued that now was simply not a good time to engage in major systemic change.

Under this scenario, then, the NCNP would not want the ULD to break away from the coalition to ally itself with the opposition and push for a constitutional change. For this reason, the NCNP itself would want to secure at least one hundred seats in the national assembly to block the ULD's potential attempt to amend the constitution—that is, if the NCNP did not want to honor its previous agreement with the ULD. At the time Kim Dae-jung came in as the new president, the NCNP controlled only seventy-eight seats. This meant that the governing party needed to come up with a political reform measure that could ensure that it gained the needed seats.[2]

Alternative Electoral Institutions

As the above section has shown, the NCNP had several objectives, stated and unstated, for the political reform. The proposed political reform included electoral reform, party reform, and reform in the practices of the national assembly, among other things (*Joongang Ilbo,* February 28, June 23, July 2, 1998). My focus in this chapter is electoral reform, and I will assess whether different electoral institutions could have achieved both the stated and unstated objectives of the NCNP's political reform. To do so, I will first review alternative electoral institutions proposed by various actors in Korea:

1. A proportional representation (PR) system with large districts,[3] proposed by the Central Election Management Committee.
2. A 200-member national assembly, based on the plurality rule with multimember districts (MMDs),[4] proposed by Chonkyongryon (National Association of Businesspersons).
3. A 250-member national assembly, based on a German-style mixed electoral system, initially proposed by the governing NCNP. Under the proposed system, one-half of the national assembly members would be elected in single-member districts (SMDs), with the remaining one-half PR seats selected in six large districts. The three-SMD-seats rule and a minimum threshold of 5 percent of the list votes apply (see below).

Since the governing NCNP once stated that the German system suited Korea, we need to find out more about it. The German electoral system combines single-member districts with proportional representation. The German voter casts two votes, a ballot for a candidate in a single-member district (called *Erststimme*) and another for a party list (called *Zweitstimme*). One-half of the Bundestag is made up of those elected in SMDs by plurality vote. The remaining half is composed from the party lists in such a way that the overall composition of the Bundestag reflects the outcome of the *Zweitstimme*. To prevent a proliferation of small parties, no party is allowed seats in the Bundestag unless it either wins seats in three SMDs or it gains at least 5 percent of the overall list votes (see Kitzinger 1960; Conradt 1970; Fisher 1973; and Barnes et al. 1992 for greater details about the German electoral system).

We need to note that in the Bundestag, the PR portion of the seats is distributed among parties *in such a way that the overall composition of the Bundestag reflects the outcome of the Zweitstimme*. This means that the Bundestag looks as if it is entirely based on the party list, the *Zweitstimme*, as long as there are no parties that acquire a disproportionately large or small number of seats in SMDs compared to the party list vote. In this case, then, Alternative 3 above is nearly identical to Alternative 1 when the same PR districts are adopted and the size of the national assembly stays constant.

4. A 250-member national assembly based on a purely mixed electoral system.[5] The governing NCNP switched from its initial position and advocated this system in late 1998. Under this system, one-half of the national assembly members would be elected in single-member districts, with the remaining one-half PR seats selected in six large districts.[6] The three-SMD-seats rule and a minimum threshold of 5 percent of the list votes would apply.

Under the pure mixed system, the seats acquired from the SMDs and the PR districts are simply added together to determine a party's overall representation in the parliament. Rather than the German system, this is more in line with the new Japanese system, in which 300 members are elected in single-member districts and 200 PR seats are selected in eleven large districts to make up a 500-member Diet.

Two additional electoral systems will likely exhaust the more common forms of electoral institutions that are adopted in democratic societies, and probably most electoral institutions ever proposed by some political group in recent Korean history.[7] They are:

5. A proportional representation system with a nationwide constituency.[8]
6. An SMD system.[9]

Estimating Seat Distribution within the National Assembly

In this section, I attempt to predict the electoral consequences of various electoral institutions introduced in the previous section. Among the proposed alternatives, it is simply impossible to gauge the impact of the plurality system with multimember districts (Alternative 2 above) since its impact would depend on the size of the districts and how they were drawn once this alternative was chosen, information simply not available at this point. As pointed out above, Alternative 3 (a modified German system) would result in an election result very similar to that of Alternative 1. Korea has already adopted a minimally modified version of the SMD system (Alternative 6), and the seat distribution in the elective seats column of table 5.1 is a good indicator of election outcome under the SMD system.[10] Therefore, my efforts in this section will focus on estimating the impact of a PR system with large districts, a modified Japanese mixed system, and a PR system with a nationwide constituency, Alternatives 1, 4, and 5 above.

To estimate the number of seats controlled by individual parties under different electoral institutions, I assume that the level of party support within regions fluctuates only marginally across elections. This has proved to be the case in the past. Based on this assumption, I use the outcomes of past elections to estimate future election results.[11] I relax this assumption and explore its impact in the last section of this chapter.

Table 5.1. The Results of the National Assembly Elections in 1996.

Parties	Elective seats	At-large seats	Total
NCNP	66	13	79
ULD	41	9	50
NKP	121	18	139*
DP	9	6	15*
Independents	16	n/a	16*
Total	253	46	299

* After the elections, the then-governing New Korea Party (NKP) secured a simple majority of seats (150) in the national assembly by absorbing most of the national assemblymen elected as independents. It merged itself with the Democratic Party (DP) to create an even larger and new governing party called the Grand National Party (GNP) shortly before the presidential elections of 1997.

When the Kim government contemplated electoral system change, the three latest elections in which the whole electorate of Korea participated were the 1996 national assembly elections, the 1997 presidential election, and the 1998 local government elections, in which governors and mayors as well as members of local assemblies were selected. The statistics from these elections, therefore, constitute natural candidates for the bases of the estimation of future election results.[12] Among these three sets of election results, I choose to use those of the 1996 national assembly elections and the 1998 local government elections, but not the 1997 presidential election.

The reason why I dropped the 1997 presidential election is that a group of national assemblymen broke away from the then-governing Grand National Party and formed the New Party by the People (NPP) only a few weeks prior to the scheduled presidential election in December 1997. It fielded its own presidential candidate, Rhee In-je, a former governor of Gyonggi province. As a candidate for a brand new party, Rhee performed rather well, garnering 19.2 percent of the total votes cast nationwide. His performance was based on his personal popularity rather than the electoral strength of the party he represented, which held eight seats in the 299-member national assembly. In fact, the party itself was created to accommodate Rhee's presidential bid when he decided to break away from the GNP. The huge disparity between the level of support he generated and the proportion of seats his party controlled (2.68 percent of the seats in the national assembly) warrants biased results if the estimate of the party's future electoral support is based on Rhee's performance in the presidential elections.

I first estimated the seat distribution in the national assembly under the proportional representation system with a single nationwide district, based on the past results from the 1996 national assembly elections and the 1998 local government elections. I calculated the proportion of nationwide votes received by individual parties in the two elections respectively and then multiplied them by the total number of seats in the national assembly, namely 299.[13] Given the fact that the governing NCNP advocated downsizing the institution, I also estimated the seat distribution under the alternative size of the national assembly, 250. The minimum threshold of 5 percent of total votes cast was applied. The results of this estimation are presented in table 5.2.

Second, I estimated the seat distribution within the national assembly

Table 5.2. Projected Seat Distribution under PR System with a Nationwide District.

Parties/stats	1996 national assembly elections	1998 local elections
NCNP	87 (73)	166 (138)*
ULD	55 (46)	–
GNP	157 (131)	133 (112)
Total	299 (250)	299 (250)

* The NCNP-ULD coalition jointly fielded their candidates for the 1998 local elections to avoid overlapping of candidates. This makes each party's nationwide vote total less meaningful. Therefore, I treated the coalition as if it were a single party and came up with the number of seats for the two parties combined.

under the alternative institution of proportional representation with large districts. I first divided the whole country into six large districts, using the NCNP's districting plan.[14]

Next, I calculated the number of seats available for these districts based on population size. I then assigned the seats to individual parties in each district, in proportion to their performance in that district in the two previous elections. Finally, I added the seats each party acquired in all districts to get that party's share of seats in the national assembly. The minimum threshold of 5 percent of total votes cast was applied. The results of this estimation are presented in table 5.3.

Finally, I estimated the national assembly seat distribution under a mixed electoral system in which one-half of the 250-member assembly was elected in SMDs and the remaining half was elected in six large districts by proportional representation. The PR seats were determined as above. That is, I calculated the number of seats available for these districts

Table 5.3. Projected Seat Distribution under PR System with Six Large Districts.

Parties/stats	1996 national assembly elections	1998 local elections
NCNP	80 (70)	158 (132)*
ULD	57 (47)	–
GNP	162 (133)	141 (118)
Total	299 (250)	299 (250)

* The NCNP-ULD coalition jointly fielded their candidates for the 1998 local elections to avoid overlapping of candidates. This makes each party's nationwide vote total less meaningful. Therefore, I treated the coalition as if it were a single party and came up with the number of seats for the two parties combined.

Table 5.4. Projected Seat Distribution under a Mixed System.

Parties/stats	1996 national assembly elections	1998 local elections
NCNP	68 (35 + 33)	121 (56 + 65)*
ULD	45 (22 + 23)	–
GNP	137 (68 + 69)	129 (69 + 60)
Total	250 (125 + 125)	250 (125 + 125)

* I can only get the number of PR seats for the NCNP and the ULD combined, 65, utilizing the 1998 local election results. It was added to the predicted number of SMD seats for the two parties to produce the total number of the national assembly seats for the two parties combined.

based on population size and the total PR seats of 125. I then assigned the seats to individual parties in each district, in proportion to their performance in that district in the two previous elections. Finally, I added the seats each party acquired in all districts to get that party's share of PR seats in the national assembly. The minimal threshold of 5 percent of total votes cast was applied.

Having obtained the number of PR seats for each party, my next task was to estimate individual parties' performance in the SMD portion of the mixed system. In estimating the number of seats obtained by each party, I assumed that it was proportional to the number of elective seats obtained by that party in the national assembly elections of 1996. Given my earlier assumption that the level of party support within regions would stay consistent across elections, and in the absence of information about how the future districts would be drawn under this new electoral system with 125 SMDs, I used the best available source of information in estimating the number of SMD seats that each party would acquire. The results of this estimation are presented in table 5.4. Each number in the table represents the predicted number of seats for each party, with the predicted number of SMD seats and PR seats in parentheses.

The NCNP's Objectives and Electoral Institutions

I have examined the estimated consequences of the three electoral institutions above. Before I address whether they achieve the objectives set out by the NCNP, I will add an observation about an alternative not examined in this chapter, the plurality system with MMDs (Alternative 2 above). It was not examined here because the necessary information is simply not available at this point. It has been shown by political scientists, however, that parties with concentrated support tend to benefit from the SMD system, while parties with broad support benefit from MMDs (Gudgin and Taylor 1979; Taagepera and Shugart 1989; see Brady and Mo 1992 for an application of this argument to Korean political parties). As I will discuss below, the governing NCNP had a geographically concentrated (but intense) support base, while the opposition GNP had a much broader support base. The point here is that although the plurality system with MMDs is not examined in this chapter, it may not matter since it is the system the governing NCNP wanted to avoid anyway.[15]

Now I evaluate how well the three alternative electoral institutions examined in this chapter would have achieved both the stated and unstated objectives of the NCNP's political reform. As I stated above, a modified German system (Alternative 3) would have an impact similar to a PR system with large districts. An SMD system (Alternative 6) can be considered the status quo here (see the elective seats column of table 5.1). The downsizing of the national assembly from its 299 members is possible under all three alternatives, which would lower the cost both of the electoral process and of running the national assembly. This would achieve the first of the NCNP's publicly stated objectives.

It is generally agreed among political scientists that the proportional representation system reflects public opinion more thoroughly than the SMD system, since most minority opinions are likely to be represented in some fashion under the PR system (see, for example, Bogdanor 1983; Vowles 1995; Cohen 1997). All three systems examined either would add a PR component to the existing system or replace it with a total PR system. Therefore, we can say that all three alternatives somehow would reflect public opinion better than the existing and primarily SMD system, thus achieving the second of the NCNP's stated objectives.

The third objective of the NCNP's political reform stated above was transforming the party to one with nationwide support. The NCNP (or its predecessor, the Party for Peace and Democracy, also led by Kim Dae-jung) had primarily represented the southwestern provinces of Cholla and, to a lesser degree, the capital Seoul-Gyonggi-Inchon region, where many people from Cholla live.[16] With the added PR component in all three alternatives examined above, it was likely that the NCNP would gain seats outside of Cholla provinces and the Seoul-Gyonggi region, however few they would turn out to be. This would add some "national flavor" to the party's regional character. So we can say that all three electoral institutions examined here would help achieve the NCNP's first three objectives to a certain degree.

Now I examine how well these alternatives would satisfy the two remaining objectives stated above. Examining tables 5.2 through 5.4, we find that there is little variation in the performance of political parties across different electoral systems when the results of the 1996 national assembly elections are used to predict party performance. The individual parties receive a quite similar number of seats regardless of the electoral rules used. Another conspicuous observation is that it is the opposition GNP, and not the NCNP-ULD coalition, which secures the majority of seats in the national assembly under all three electoral rules examined. The GNP acquires 157 to 162 seats in the 299-member assembly (where 150 constitutes a majority) in tables 5.2 and 5.3. It acquires 131 to 137 seats in the 250-member assembly (where 126 constitutes a majority) in tables 5.2 to 5.4. The situation is somewhat different when the results of the 1998 local elections are used as a proxy for future performance. The coalition of the NCNP and the ULD secures a majority in PR systems (158 to 166 seats in the 299-member assembly and 132 to 138 in the 250-member assembly), while the GNP secures a majority in the mixed system with 129 seats out of 250.

At first, it looks surprising that the NCNP and the ULD, with their more concentrated geographical support than the GNP, actually perform better in the PR systems than the mixed system when we use the results of the local elections. I believe the answer is in these parties' electoral strategy. For the local elections of 1998, the NCNP and the ULD jointly fielded candidates for governors and mayors to avoid overlapping their candidates in the same provinces or specially administered cities. Whichever party had an edge in the province was asked to nominate a candidate for that province. This means that these two parties acted as if they were a single party. In this way, these parties fielded the most competitive candidate in each province. The result of my examination above shows, then, that, although these parties were more geographically concentrated than the GNP *individually*, they *collectively* appealed to a broader segment of the electorate than the GNP.

The question is whether this kind of cooperation between the NCNP and the ULD was feasible in the next national assembly elections if indeed a PR system were adopted. This kind of cooperation amounts to one of the parties' not presenting a slate of candidates for some provinces where the other party is stronger. It amounts to one of them not seeking any national assembly seats if a nationwide district is adopted. As anyone would agree, this kind of cooperation was highly improbable. Even a compromise solution of a mixed slate between the two parties for some districts would take an extreme level of coordination. In sum, given the results presented in tables 5.2 through 5.4 and the implausibility of the kind of cooperation necessary under the PR system, we are left pessimistic about the NCNP-ULD coalition's chances of achieving a stable majority within the national assembly under *any* kind of electoral system, including the existing (primarily) SMD system (see table 5.1).

How about the NCNP's last objective of preventing an opposition party, in this case, the GNP, from acquiring one-third of the seats in the national assembly, or guaranteeing that the NCNP itself acquires one-third of the seats? One-third of the seats amounts to 100 seats in the 299-member national assembly, or 84 in the 250-member assembly. A cursory look at the three tables above shows that no matter which electoral system is adopted, the NCNP simply cannot prevent the GNP from acquiring one-third of the seats in the assembly given the latter's support base. As the tables show, the GNP *always* secures much more than one-third of the seats. About the NCNP's own attempt at securing one-third of the seats, my results based on the 1996 national assembly election results give a rather pessimistic diagnosis. It is impossible to tell using the 1998 local election results, since we cannot distinguish the NCNP seats from the ULD seats.

I now sum up the findings in this chapter. The Kim government and the NCNP proposed a series of political reforms in 1998. The electoral institutions examined in this chapter seem to have been able to achieve, to a certain degree, the NCNP's stated objectives of lowering the cost of elections, producing a more accurate reflection of public opinion, and transforming itself into a party with nationwide appeal. My findings in the previous two sections show, however, that it was highly unlikely, under any electoral system, that the NCNP achieved its more important goal of allowing the governing NCNP-ULD coalition a stable majority in the national assembly. Further, it is shown that an equally pressing objective of preventing the opposition GNP from controlling over one-third of the seats in the national assembly or allowing the NCNP itself to control that many would be almost impossible, under any electoral institutions, including the existing (primarily) SMD system.

So the verdict is in and the message is clear. The NCNP's last two objectives of political reform were simply not compatible with any of the proposed democratic forms of electoral institutions. *Electoral reform was simply insufficient to achieve these objectives.*

Discussion

In 1998, the governing party politicians began to stress the need for "the reorganization of the political circle (*jeonggye gaepyun*)" on top of "political reform." As abstract as the term "reorganization" can be, the NCNP's version of "the reorganization" turned out to be any or all of the following: (1) somehow inducing the opposition GNP assemblymen to change their party affiliation to either the NCNP or the ULD; or (2) somehow causing a split within the GNP so that some portion of it would leave the party to form a new political party; or (3) somehow forcing corrupt GNP assemblymen to either voluntarily or involuntarily retire from politics altogether.

How did these seemingly incredible events occur? In the spring of 1998, newspapers began to report that government prosecutors had uncovered a corruption ring involving failing corporations and politicians. Rumors surfaced that the prosecutors had made up a list of corrupt politicians, and that inquiry into their finances was imminent. The government prosecutors actually acted on these threats by charging and/or arresting several assemblymen in September 1998. Interestingly, the politicians already under investigation by the government prosecutors and those rumored to be on the "black list" were predominantly GNP assemblymen. The opposition accused the NCNP of using government prosecutors to intimidate the GNP members so that they would leave the party. In a survey of the general public carried out by *Joongang Ilbo* in September 1998, over half of the respondents (50.8 percent) agreed that the government investigation of politicians was aimed at harassing and intimidating the opposition rather than a fair application of the rule of law (*Joongang Ilbo,* September 22, 1998).

Since Kim Dae-jung took office and by the time the "reorganization" efforts ended, two GNP assemblymen had died, three had lost their seats after having been found guilty of various charges, six had resigned (some of them to run for other offices), twenty-seven had changed their party affiliation (eighteen to the NCNP and nine to the ULD), and two had

Table 5.5. The National Assembly Seat Distribution as of September 1999.

Parties	Number of seats
NCNP	105
ULD	55
GNP	133
Independents	5
Total	298*

* A GNP assemblyman resigned in September 1999 for his role in the illegal contribution gathering scheme during the presidential election campaign in 1997. The supplementary election had not yet taken place.

broken away from the party to become independents (*Joongang Ilbo,* various dates, 1998, 1999).[17] On August 29, 1998, the NCNP and the NPP announced the merger of their parties. For all practical purposes, however, the latter was absorbed by the former, and the NPP disappeared after only ten months of existence. Of the eight NPP national assemblymen, one chose to join the ULD instead of the NCNP and one became an independent (*Joongang Ilbo,* September 1, 1998). Table 5.5 shows the seat distribution within the national assembly after these events and represents a significant change from table 5.1. The number of seats held by the NCNP and the ULD combined was over the simple majority mark (with 160), and the NCNP had secured more than one-third of the seats in the national assembly, all without electoral reform!

Two comments are in order here. First, ever since its democratic opening in 1987, Korea had gradually democratized its political processes, culminating in the first-ever peaceful change of government from one party to another in the history of the country, through direct elections in 1997. The Kim Dae-jung government came into power as a result and declared itself to be "the people's government." In its first year in power, however, the Kim government embarked on "reorganization," which basically nullified the results of the 1996 national assembly elections.

It is generally assumed in studies of institutions and democratic transitions that political actors have many goals and objectives that go into their calculus of institutional choice at the time they bargain for new institutional arrangements. As we saw above, the governing NCNP had several stated and unstated objectives of political reform. In the seeming absence of an electoral institution that could simultaneously and feasibly satisfy its objectives, the Kim Dae-jung government appears to have opted for the quick fix of political reorganization.[18]

The second point to be made here is about the applicability of the rational choice paradigm to Korean situations and third-world politics in general. As I mentioned above, the reorganization effort nullified the results of the 1996 national assembly elections, and thus entailed a certain level of risk that had to be borne on the part of the Kim government and the NCNP. The fact that they nevertheless pushed for the reorganization implies (1) that there had been a certain kind of calculation, on the part of the governing party, of the feasibility of achieving its objectives of political reform through democratic means, such as electoral reform, the kind of calculation included in this chapter; and (2) that they also concluded, as I did in this chapter, that their more important objectives would not be satisfied merely by implementing electoral reform. I do not mean that they did exactly the same calculation that I did in this chapter, or that they used exactly the same election statistics that I used to predict the future electoral consequences of different kinds of electoral institutions. I simply mean that it appears there was some kind of calculation and a conclusion based on that calculation. This further implies that the government's action was based on rational expectations. They attempted to use available information to weigh their options and chose the best means to achieve their objectives (van Winden 1988; see Brady and Mo 1992 and Kim and Kim 1995 for representative applications of rational choice theory to Korean politics).

If they concluded that reorganization was necessary to achieve their objectives, then it was entirely rational for the NCNP to attempt reorganization *before* political reform. As mentioned above, the reorganization included inducing the opposition GNP assemblymen to change their party affiliation to the NCNP. Also, voter support for the NCNP primarily came from Cholla provinces and the capital region. Many of the GNP assemblymen who crossed the party line represented districts outside of the NCNP's strongholds. This would have the effect of expanding the party's support base, assuming that these incumbents continued to garner the level of support they generated in previous elections.[19]

New Political Issues in 1999 and Beyond

In their negotiation with the ULD about electoral reform in 1999, leaders of the NCNP indicated their willingness to accept a mixed electoral system that had not been discussed previously. Under this system, a certain percentage of the national assembly members would be elected, using plurality rule, in MMDs (2–3 members per district), with the remaining seats selected through PR in six large districts (*Joongang Ilbo,* May 26, 1999). First of all, this was a rather unique system. It is known among political scientists that the SMD system tends to produce a stable political system with a handful of (if not just two) parties and often with a majority party. Its weakness is the lack of proportionality—that is, the proportion of votes parties receive does not always translate into a comparable proportion of seats in the parliament. The PR system best approximates a party's electoral support to its level of representation but tends to create a large number of parties, and oftentimes an unstable political system.[20] The plurality system with MMDs inherently has some characteristics of both PR and SMDs. Therefore, a mixed system of the plurality-rule MMDs and PR was rather unusual.

Second, the fact that the NCNP was willing to accept the plurality system with MMDs as part of the electoral package was a rather dramatic turnaround, given their narrow and concentrated support base in previous elections. This may indeed have reflected the NCNP's estimate of its expanded support base through the absorption of the GNP assemblymen. It may also have reflected the two factors mentioned in note 5.11, which are not analyzed in this chapter. Namely, in the 2000 national assembly election the leaders of the NCNP could expect to have incumbent advantage, as the business community would be more prone to contribute to, and the local bureaucrats would be more willing to work with, the governing party. Furthermore, there was a common perception that the Korean economy was reviving from the devastating crisis of 1997 and 1998, and it was widely accepted that the Kim government's economic policies were at least partially responsible (*Joongang Ilbo,* February 24, 1999). As discussed earlier, this good performance in office would expand the level of support for the governing party, and it might be able to win more votes at the margin.

6

Uncertainty in Foreign Policy Making

Changing Relations among South Korea, North Korea, and the United States of America in the Twenty-First Century

Bayesian (incomplete information) games are used to analyze situations where at least one player is uncertain about the others' preferences. For the past decade or so, Bayesian models have been rigorously applied to various aspects of international relations involving uncertainty. They include international conflict, alliance formation, deterrence, domestic constraints on foreign policy, as well as reputation building in the world political economy.[1]

These models have contributed to our understanding of international relations by uncovering complicated strategic interactions through deductive reasoning and by generating many empirically testable hypotheses. Apart from these efforts for general theory developments, however, scholars have rarely applied Bayesian models to analyze real-world international events, although many of them involve situations where one or more players are uncertain about the others' preferences. Some of these events are interesting and important in their own right, given their potential impact on regional security and the amount of attention paid by scholars and politicians alike. Therefore, these cases warrant independent studies utilizing Bayesian models.

One such situation would be the changing relationships North Korea has with South Korea and the United States. As I will demonstrate in the following section, both South Korean and U.S. policy makers have attempted to formulate their new North Korea policies while they were uncertain about the true intentions of the North Korean leadership, especially since the late 1990s. One potential payoff of developing Bayesian games of a real-world situation such as that on the Korean peninsula is that one can make predictions and policy recommendations specific to the situation and observe empirically how the players act as the situation unfolds. Another aspect of North Korea–South Korea–United States relations that makes them interesting is that the North Korean leadership is simultaneously playing similar, but separate, games with South Korea and the United States. If the North sends a certain signal (reveals its intentions) in one game, its competitor in the other will try to use that information as well. This necessarily constrains the North Korean choice of strategies, as I will demonstrate below.[2]

In the first section of this chapter, I discuss the changing political situations on the Korean peninsula. By doing so, I also establish that the situation is amenable to Bayesian game analysis. In the two following sections, I present the Bayesian games between North Korea and South Korea, and North Korea and the United States, respectively. After solving for the equilibria of these games, I discuss the insights and substantive implications these models provide.

The Changing Political Situations on the Korean Peninsula

In June 2000, the North Korean leader, Kim Jong-il, accepted South Korean president Kim Dae-jung's call for a South-North summit. The first-ever summit of the two Koreas' leaders was held in the North Korean capital of Pyongyang, followed by the visits of separated families and the flow of South Korean capital across the border. This rapprochement culminated at the Sydney Olympics, when the athletes from the two Koreas walked together under one flag in the opening ceremony. This was a dramatic and quite unexpected turn of events, since the North Korean regime and Kim Jong-il had been known for their aggressiveness, inflexibility, and unwillingness to compromise with the outside world. These events also prompted the Clinton administration to reassess its North Korea policy, leading to U.S. Secretary of State Madeleine Albright's visit to Pyongyang (*Hankuk Ilbo,* December 14, 2000, June 9, 2001).

There are two competing explanations for the North's change of mind. First, the North Korean leaders have come to accept that the only way out of poverty and isolation is to open up the country's border to the South and to the United States, accepting the inevitability of systemic and structural reform (see, for example, Kim 2002). The second possibility is that this is an attempt to take advantage of outside aid and lower tensions on the Korean peninsula temporarily, until the North recovers from its economic problems. Thus, the North's change would be a short-term strategic move rather than a long-term fundamental change (see, for example, an editorial in the *New York Times*, October 15, 2000, and Kim 2002).[3]

Obviously, the South's and the United States' best courses of action differ depending on the real intentions of the North. Without complete knowledge about the North's true intentions, what would be the South's and the United States' best strategies in their interactions with the North? What would be the most likely outcome of these interactions, given the uncertainty about the North's intentions? On the North's part, it needs to be consistent about the portrayal of its intentions, since revealing its true intentions to either the South or the United States may reveal the same to the other. These are important questions for students of Korean studies as well as those of international relations. Given the uncertainty involved, however, most explanations given so far have been based on conjectures.

Bayesian game theory offers tools capable of analyzing a situation like this where at least one player is uncertain about the others' true preferences. In the following sections, I build Bayesian game-theoretic models in which the South's and United States' policy makers are uncertain about the North's true intentions. Once the North sends a signal of accommodation, as it did in 2000, the leaders of the South and the United States must determine how far they want to go in terms of accommodating back.[4]

Model 1: The South Korea–North Korea Interaction

In this section, I analyze the interaction between North Korea and South Korea, which is depicted by the extensive form in figure 6.1. There is no uncertainty about South Korea's preferences, as its leaders have consistently suggested reconciliation between the two Koreas. There are two possible types of North Korean leadership, a sincere one and a deceitful one. The sincere type truly pushes for the opening up of its border to the South (and the United States). The deceptive type attempts to take advan-

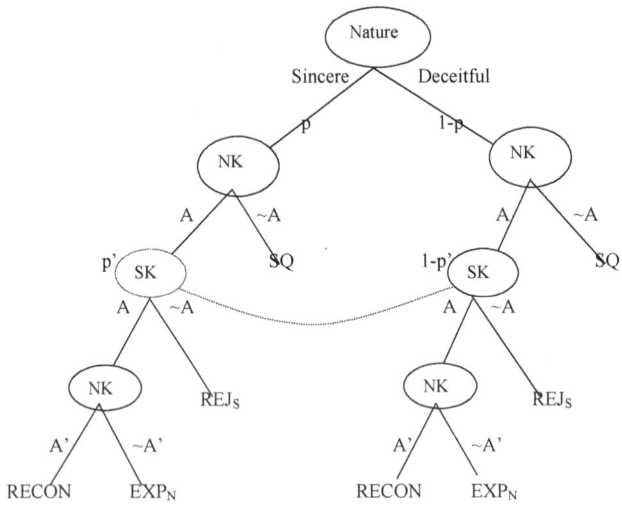

SK: U(RECON) > $U(REJ_S)$ > $U(EXP_N)$

$NK_{SINCERE}$: (RECON) > $U(EXP_N)$ > $U(REJ_S)$

$NK_{DECEITFUL}$: $U(EXP_N)$ > U(RECON) > $U(REJ_S)$

Fig. 6.1. The South Korea–North Korea Bayesian game.

tage of outside aid and lower tensions on the Korean peninsula temporarily, until the North recovers from its economic ills.

At the time of the presidential election in South Korea in 1997, then-candidate Kim Dae-jung pledged to attempt to improve relations with the North. Ever since his election, President Kim consistently maintained that his administration was open to the idea of a South-North summit and the subsequent reconciliation between the two. This was commonly known as the "Sunshine Policy." So, our game in this section begins with the North Korean response to the Kim administration's offer of the summit already on the table.

In this game, Nature moves first and determines the North's type. Then the North can *either* accept (or accommodate) South Korean president Kim Dae-jung's offer to engage *or* not. If the North does not accommodate, then the Status Quo (SQ) continues. If it chooses to accommodate, then the South gets a chance to determine whether to accommodate back fully or not. If the South somehow withdraws from its commitment to engage, then the North's accommodation is rejected by the South (REJ_S). If the South fully reciprocates and the North stops accommodating at some point in the future (~A'), then the outcome is exploitation by the North (EXP_N). If the North fully accommodates back (A'), then the outcome is reconciliation (RECON), leading toward long-term cooperation and potential unification in a peaceful manner.

As I described above, this extensive form succinctly summarizes the recent relationship between the two Koreas. For us to solve for equilibrium in this game, we first need to determine the players' preference structure. There are some assumptions about their preferences that we can make without controversy. For example, South Korea's most preferred outcome probably is RECON, while its least preferred outcome would be EXP_N. REJ_S would be in between these two outcomes. By definition, the sincere North Korea prefers RECON to EXP_N, while the deceitful North Korea prefers EXP_N to RECON. Regardless of its type, North Korea's least preferred outcome would be REJ_S. The information above leads to the following inequality conditions:

$$SK: U(RECON) > U(REJ_S) > U(EXP_N)$$
$$NK_{SINCERE}: U(RECON) > U(EXP_N) > U(REJ_S)$$
$$NK_{DECEITFUL}: U(EXP_N) > U(RECON) > U(REJ_S)$$

This leaves the location of Status Quo in relation to other possible outcomes as the only source of potential debate. For South Korea, SQ would most likely rank just ahead of REJ_S because the Kim Dae-jung government would not really gain anything by suggesting a summit and reconciliation, as it did earlier, and then backing away from it after the North accepted the offer (REJ_S). For a sincere North, SQ is probably slightly above or below EXP_N, while it is somewhere near RECON for a deceitful North. As I will demonstrate below, the location of SQ in the preference ordering of North Korea does not affect our conclusion as long as it is not the most or the least preferred outcome. With the inequality conditions above, I am now ready to solve for the equilibrium conditions. Due to its technical nature, I state the details of the equilibrium solution in appendix A.

The equilibrium solution of this game provides several insights about the North Korea–South Korea interaction. First, the North's behavior would be the same regardless of its type (Observation 1 in appendix A). That is, whether the real type of the North's leadership is sincere or deceitful, it will consistently be accommodating or consistently unaccommodating. This will make it difficult for the South to collect more information about the North's real intentions. Second, the South must continue to engage the North only if it is fairly certain that the North is truly interested in reforming its system for the long-term (Observation 2). Otherwise, the South should pull away from its initial accommodation even if it results in the loss of face on the part of the South Korean government both in and outside of the Korean peninsula. Finally, the North Korean leadership, regardless of its real type, will try to convince the South that it is sincere (Observation 3). As a matter of fact, the North did so until the change in parties in power in the United States in 2001. Why the advent of the Bush administration affected the North's behavior toward the South will be discussed in the following sections.

Model 2: The United States–North Korea Interaction

Next I build a Bayesian model in which U.S. policy makers are uncertain about the North's true intentions, as in Model 1 above. This model is more complicated than the North-South interaction, though, as there is reason to believe that North Korean policy makers are also uncertain about whether the United States truly wants eventual reconciliation with the North. Some suggested that the Bush administration could use "a threat to world peace," such as North Korea, to sell its military concept of "Missile Defense" to its allies (see for example, *Los Angeles Times,* March 8, 2001).

This situation is depicted in extensive form in figure 6.2. As before, there are two possible types of the North Korean leadership, picked by Nature, a sincere one and a deceitful one. Further, there are two possible types of the U.S. leadership, which I will call hawkish and dovish, for lack of better terms. On its first move, the North can voluntarily accommodate or not. Due to the interconnectedness of international relations situations, we can assume that this decision occurs when the North responds to the South's initial offer of a dialogue in the first game above. If they choose to accommodate, then the United States gets a chance to determine whether to accommodate back or not. If the North accommodates and the United States reciprocates, then the outcome is reconciliation ini-

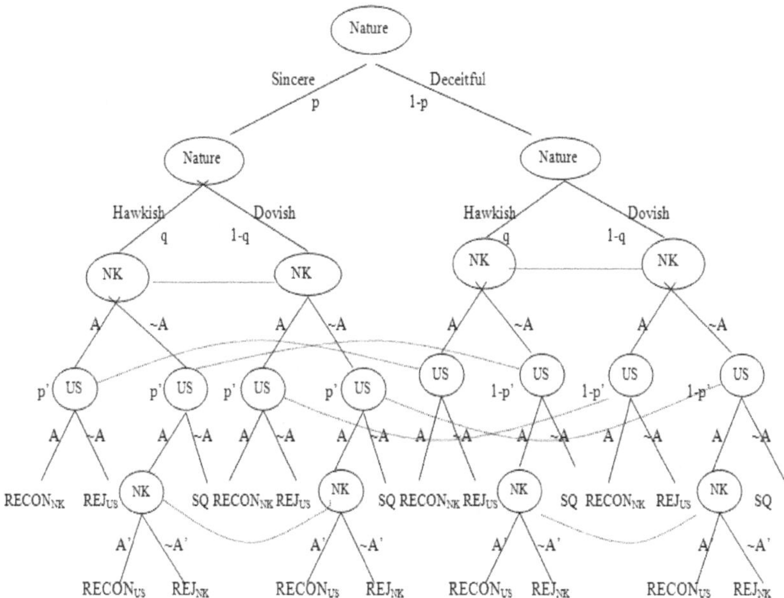

Fig. 6.2. The U.S.–North Korea Bayesian game.

tiated by the North (RECON_{NK}). If the United States does not reciprocate, then the North's accommodation is rejected by the United States (REJ_{US}). If the North does not initiate accommodation, then the United States has a choice between initiating accommodation or not. If the United States chooses not to, the outcome is Status Quo. If the United States chooses to initiate accommodation, then the North gets a chance to determine whether to accommodate back or not (A' or ~A'). If the North fully accommodates back, then the outcome is reconciliation initiated by the United States (RECON_{US}). If the North does not, the United States' offer is rejected by the North (REJ_{NK}).

For us to analyze this game, we first need to determine the players' preference structure. There are several assumptions about their preferences that we can make without much controversy. By definition, the sincere North Korea prefers the RECON outcomes to REJ_{NK}, while the deceitful North's preference over these outcomes would be reversed. Regardless of its type, the worst possible outcome for North Korea would be REJ_{US}. By definition, the hawkish United States prefers REJ_{US} or SQ to the RECON outcomes, while the situation is reversed for the dovish United States.

This leaves the location of Status Quo in relation to other possible outcomes to be determined. For the sincere North Korea, which pushes for reconciliation, Status Quo should be placed in between the RECON outcomes and REJ_{US}. For the deceitful North Korea, which does not want long-term reconciliation with the United States, Status Quo must be better than the RECON outcomes. For the hawkish United States, which does not want long-term reconciliation with North Korea, Status Quo must be preferred to the RECON outcomes. For the dovish United States, Status Quo must be placed in between the RECON outcomes and REJ_{NK}. The information in this paragraph does not give us the precise location of Status Quo in the preference ordering of all possible types of players. It does, however, along with the information above, give us enough information to be able to analyze the U.S.–North Korea relations game. The information I have presented so far can be summarized by the following inequality conditions, where a comma indicates that I do not have enough information to differentiate the two:

$$NK_{SINCERE}: RECON_{US} > RECON_{NK} > SQ, REJ_{NK} > REJ_{US}$$
$$NK_{DECEITFUL}: REJ_{NK}, SQ > RECON_{US} > RECON_{NK} > REJ_{US}$$
$$US_{HAWKISH}: REJ_{US}, SQ > RECON_{NK} > RECON_{US} > REJ_{NK}$$
$$US_{DOVISH}: RECON_{NK} > RECON_{US} > SQ, REJ_{US} > REJ_{NK}$$

With these inequality conditions, I am now ready to analyze the game. Due to its technical nature, I state the details of the analysis in appendix B. As was the case with the North Korea–South Korea Bayesian game above, the equilibrium solution of the U.S.–North Korea Bayesian game provides us with several interesting insights.

First, the hawkish United States will never initiate accommodation and will always reject the initial accommodation by North Korea (Observation 4 in appendix B). On the other hand, the dovish United States will always reciprocate the accommodation initiated by North Korea. It will also initiate accommodation in the absence of North Korea's initial accommodation, but only if it feels highly certain that North Korea is sincere (Observation 5). Third, the deceitful North Korea never initiates accommodation and will always reject the initial accommodation by the United States (Observation 6).

Observations 4–6 lead to the conclusion that long-term reconciliation between North Korea and the United States is possible *if, and only if,* North Korea is sincere about political reform and the United States is dovish toward North Korea (Observation 7). This sounds rather intuitive at first, but what I am predicting in fact is that out of eight possible RECON outcomes in figure 6.2, only two are attainable in the interaction between North Korea and the United States. Finally, the combination of the deceitful North Korea and the hawkish United States always leads to Status Quo, since neither side is willing to risk being exploited by the other (Observation 8).

U.S. Policy Toward North Korea

Shortly after the inauguration of the Bush administration in the United States, the new secretary of State, Colin Powell, announced that the U.S. government would fundamentally reexamine its North Korea policy. During the summit with President Kim Dae-jung in March 2001, U.S. president George W. Bush made it clear that the United States still considered North Korea a rogue nation and a threat to the international community, that it was too early to resume the U.S.–North Korea talks, and that any future dialogue must be based on the "complete verification" of the 1994 Geneva agreement.[5] In its annual report on terrorism in May 2001, the U.S. State Department continued to include North Korea as one of the states sponsoring terrorism.[6] Condoleezza Rice, the national security advisor for the Bush administration, stated in a White House function that Kim Jong-il was not trustworthy (*Hankuk Ilbo,* various dates, 2001).

From this information, it appears that the Bush administration's perception of the North Korean leadership was very different from that of the Kim Dae-jung government and the Clinton administration. Using the terms presented in previous sections, the Bush administration seemed to place much higher probability on the deceitful North Korean type than its predecessor and its counterpart in South Korea. However, my finding in the previous section (and Observation 4 in appendix B) indicates that the difference in the choice of actions by the Clinton administration and the Bush administration may indeed stem from the difference in their own types (preferences) and have little to do with their perceptions of North Korea.

In June 2001, President Bush signaled a change in his administration's policy toward North Korea by announcing that the United States would resume bilateral talks with Pyongyang. His proposed agenda for future talks included North Korea's nuclear development, conventional weapons deployments, and missile development. President Bush further implied potential economic aid and political cooperation with the North, contingent on the North's accommodation with the aforementioned agendas (*Hankuk Ilbo,* June 8, 2001). Secretary Colin Powell, during his visit to Seoul in July, stated that the United States was ready to talk to North Korea without preconditions. He further called on President Vladimir Putin of Russia to persuade Kim Jong-il to abandon weapons of mass destruction and resume the dialogue for peace with both South Korea and the United States (*International Herald Tribune,* July 29, 2001).

We need to note that Pyongyang did nothing to change the United States' perception of North Korea between January and June of 2001. Nevertheless, the Bush administration's North Korea policy began to change. The U.S. media interpreted this change of policy as a sign that the moderate State Department got an upper hand on the issue of North Korea over the more hawkish White House and Defense Department (see, for example, *Washington Post,* June 7, 2001). If this was indeed the case, then the change of policy was not caused by a change in U.S. policy makers' perception of North Korea, but by the change in the United States' own type from hawkish to dovish (or less hawkish)! This situation fits exactly with what our model is telling us (Observations 4 and 5). The United States' perception of North Korea (or the United States' type), however, took another turn when President Bush defined North Korea as part of the "axis of evil," along with Iran and Iraq, in his state of the union address in January 2002, following the 9/11 terrorist attack on America (see the last section of this chapter).

The Simultaneous Nature of the Two Games

As I mentioned above, North Korea is playing the two separate games simultaneously. The dilemma it faces is that it is not flexible in its choice of strategies (and thus, in its attempt to portray itself as sincere) since an opponent in one game can observe the North Korean choice of actions in the other game.[7] For example, it is in the best interest of the North Korean leadership to portray itself as a true reformer in its game with South Korea

(Observation 3). The same is not necessarily the case in the U.S.–North Korea interaction (Observation 6). Nevertheless, due to the simultaneous and observable nature of the two games, the North Korean leadership cannot portray itself to be two conflicting types in two separate games. This means that if the relationship strains and the negotiations stall in one game, the same is likely to happen in the other. This is exactly what happened in early 2001. That is, when the U.S.–North Korea dialogue stalled, North Korea also stopped responding to the South Korean gesture for continuous dialogue. The North Korean leadership further toughened its stance in August. After a summit in Moscow, Kim Jong-il and Russia's President Putin reiterated their old argument that the withdrawal of U.S. forces from South Korea was critical for peace and security in the Korean peninsula and northeast Asia (*Joongang Ilbo,* August 6, 2002).[8]

The simultaneous nature of the two games analyzed in this chapter and the restraint on the North Korean leadership in their choice of strategies explains why President Bush's announcement to engage North Korea again received more public and positive response from South Korea than the North (*Hankuk Ilbo,* June 8, 2001). The South Korean leadership understood that once the negotiations resumed between the United States and North Korea, the same thing would happen between North Korea and South Korea.

Discussion

In this chapter I studied the changing relationships North Korea has with South Korea and the United States. As I demonstrated above, both South Korean and U.S. policy makers attempted to formulate their new North Korea policies while they were uncertain about the true intentions of the North Korean leadership, especially since the late 1990s. By applying Bayesian games to the Korean situation, we can make some very interesting observations.

In the interaction between North Korea and South Korea, for example, the North will be consistently accommodating or consistently unaccommodating regardless of whether it truly wants change or not. This will make it difficult for the South to collect more information about the real intentions of the North Korean leadership. I recommend that the South must continue to engage the North only if it strongly believes that the North is truly interested in reforming its system for the long-term. Otherwise, Seoul should pull away from its initial accommodation even if it results in the loss of face on the part of the South Korean government. Finally, I expect that the North Korean leadership, regardless of its real intentions, will try to convince the South that it is sincere. We will continue to see North Korea attempt to gesture its willingness to reform as long as there is no uncertainty about the South's type.

In the interaction between North Korea and the United States, I expect that the hawkish United States will never initiate accommodation and will always reject the initial accommodation by North Korea. On the other hand, the dovish United States will always reciprocate the accommodation initiated by North Korea. It will also initiate accommodation in the absence of North Korea's initial accommodation, but only when it feels highly certain that North Korea truly desires change. The deceitful North Korea never initiates accommodation and will always reject the initial accommodation by the United States. Based on these observations, I predict that the long-term reconciliation between North Korea and the United States is possible *if, and only if,* North Korea is sincere about reform and the United States is dovish toward North Korea. Further, the combination of the deceitful North Korea and the hawkish United States always leads to Status Quo, since neither side is willing to risk being exploited by the other.

As I discussed above, the George W. Bush administration in the United States toughened its policy toward North Korea, citing that it perceived the latter as a threat to world peace. By all indications, the Bush administration seemed to place much higher probability on the deceitful North Korean type than its predecessor and its counterpart in South Korea. In June of 2001, however, the U.S. government softened its policy toward North Korea by announcing its willingness to engage North Korea without preconditions. I believe that this change in U.S. policy toward North Korea was caused by the change in the United States' own type, as my model indicates, and as some media coverage reported, rather than a change in the Bush administration's perception of the North Korean regime.

Another aspect of North Korea–South Korea–United States relations that makes them interesting is that the North Korean leadership with private information about its real intentions is simultaneously playing two separate games, one with South Korea and the other with the United States. The dilemma it faces is that it is not flexible in its choice of strategies (and thus, its attempt to portray itself as sincere) since an opponent in one game can observe the North Korean choice of actions in the other game. For example, it is in the best interest of the North Korean leadership to portray itself as a true reformer in its game with South Korea (Observation 3). The same is not necessarily the case in the U.S.–North Korea interaction (Observation 6). Nevertheless, due to the simultaneous and observable nature of the two games, the North Korean leadership cannot portray itself to be two conflicting types in two separate games. This means that if the relationship strains and the negotiations stall in one game, the same is likely to happen in the other, as happened in 2001 when the U.S.–North Korea stalemate caused the North Korea–South Korea relationship to strain as well.

Postscript

There was no uncertainty about the South's preferences under the Kim Dae-jung government, as its leaders consistently suggested reconciliation between the two Koreas. This assuredness about the South Korean position was in doubt during the 2002 presidential campaign, however. With President Kim Dae-jung's term scheduled to end in early 2003, public opinion polls consistently showed the governing party candidate, Roh Moo-hyun, trailing the opposition candidate, Lee Hoi-chang (Grand National Party). The opposition had been quite critical of the Kim government's reconciliation policy and had promised to take a more conservative approach toward the North.[9] Pyongyang knew that if Lee Hoi-chang were to win the presidential election, South Korea's policy toward the North would most likely change. This created uncertainty as to what path the future South Korean government would take regarding cooperation with the North. This meant that neither side would be certain about the other's intentions in the interaction between North and South Korea, a situation more complicated than the one depicted in figure 6.1. As before, there would be two possible types of the North Korean leadership picked by Nature, a sincere one and a deceitful one. Further, there would be two possible types of South Korean leadership, which might be called hawkish and dovish.

This uncertainty about the preferences of the future South Korean government all but evaporated in the December 2002 presidential election, when the governing party candidate, Roh Moo-hyun, defeated Lee

Hoi-chang in what was widely viewed as a stunning upset (see the next chapter). In an interview with *Le Monde,* president-elect Roh Moo-hyun stated that the "Sunshine Policy" was the only feasible alternative for inter-Korean relations (*Joongang Ilbo,* various dates, 2002).

On the other hand, the Bush administration's preferences/perceptions took the other direction following the 9/11 terrorist attack. President Bush defined North Korea as part of the "axis of evil," along with Iran and Iraq, in his state of the union address in January 2002. In March the U.S. State Department placed North Korea, along with Iran and Iraq, on its list of the world's worst violators of human rights. The State Department's 2002 human rights report specifically denounced the North for its propensity to resort to "extrajudicial killings and disappearances" (*Korea Focus,* March–April 2002). In May, it maintained its designation of North Korea as a state sponsor of terrorism, along with Iran, Sudan, Libya, Iraq, Cuba, and Syria (*Korea Focus,* May–June, 2002).

In early October 2002, the U.S. undersecretary of state, James Kelly, visited North Korea. When pressed by Kelly, the North Korean senior vice premier, Kang Suk-ju, admitted that North Korea had maintained its nuclear weapons development program based on the uranium enhancement method. In a meeting with the South Korean unification minister in late October, Kim Young-nam, the chair of the standing committee of the North Korean National People's Congress (the nominal head of state), stated that North Korea was willing to resolve security issues through dialogue if the United States was willing to move away from its hostile North Korea policy. The U.S. government stated that negotiations with the North should be preceded by the latter's abandonment of its nuclear development programs, which North Korea rejected.

In November 2002, the Korean Peninsula Energy Development Organization, composed of South Korea, the United States, Japan, and the European Union decided to halt its supply of heavy fuel oil to North Korea beginning in December. In response, North Korea announced its intention to restart its nuclear reactors, whose operation had been frozen under the Geneva agreement. (These reactors are capable of producing the plutonium necessary to develop nuclear weapons.) In the meantime, somewhat mixed signals were coming out of the U.S. government, probably reflecting two different sets of preferences. On December 23, 2002, the U.S. Secretary of Defense, Donald Rumsfeld, stated that the United States was capable of fighting two wars simultaneously, one against Iraq and the other against North Korea. On the other hand, reactions of the State Department were rather different. Secretary Powell stated on December 16 that the United States was prepared to improve relations with North Korea based on the latter's abandonment of its nuclear programs.

In late December, North Korea, contrary to the Geneva agreement, broke the seals on its nuclear reactors and the eight thousand spent plutonium fuel rods. At the same time, the North Korean government expelled the International Atomic Energy Agency inspectors who had been in the country to oversee its nuclear freeze (*Joong-ang Ilbo,* various dates, 2002). In January 2003, North Korea withdrew from the Nuclear Non-Proliferation Treaty.

As the Bush administration adopted hawkish policies in security issues in general, and North Korea continued to pursue its nuclear strategy leading to the nuclear weapons tests and missile test launches, it became obvious that any kind of reconciliation outcome in figure 6.2 was out of reach.

7

A Risky Game to Play

The Politics of the Impeachment Game in 2004

On March 12, 2004, a stunning political event happened in South Korea when its national assembly impeached President Roh Moo-hyun, only a year into his term as president. The opposition parties, with over two-thirds of the seats in the assembly, decided to use their numerical strength only one month before the next national assembly elections. As a result of the impeachment, the case was sent to the Constitutional Court for a final decision according to the Korean constitution. Roh's presidential powers were immediately suspended, and Prime Minister Koh Gun became acting head of state. The opposition's reason for the impeachment was the president's public expression of support for the governing Woori Party for the upcoming national assembly elections (which oddly enough was a violation of election law in Korea) and his refusal to publicly apologize for his conduct as the opposition demanded (*Hankuk Ilbo,* various dates, 2004).

Why did President Roh refuse to accept the opposition's demand for an apology and take the risk of impeachment, knowing that the opposition had a sufficient number of votes? Also, why did the opposition go ahead and impeach the president for seemingly trivial reasons at the risk of punishment by the electorate, with the national assembly elections only a month away? These are puzzling questions, since neither side seemed to have acted in a rational fashion. This situation is further complicated since neither side knew with certainty whether the Constitutional Court would uphold the impeachment and how the electorate would react to the impeachment vote. A game-theoretic model can be used to solve these puzzles, since plenty of strategic calculations must have been involved on the part of both the president and the opposition. Further, a Bayesian (incomplete information) game-theoretic model seems appropriate, since both the president and the opposition faced the uncertainties described above.

In this chapter, I attempt to explain why the presidential impeachment took place when the choices made appear irrational to most observers of Korean politics. In the first section of this chapter, I describe the historical events leading up to and including the impeachment vote in the Korean national assembly in 2004. In the following section, I build a Bayesian game-theoretic model of the impeachment situation in Korea. Next, I describe the two political events following the impeachment, the national assembly elections and the decision by the Constitutional Court, the sources of uncertainty at the time of impeachment decision. I then evaluate the decisions made by both the president and the national assembly opposition and conclude the chapter.

Background Information

Presidential Election of 2002

The governing party candidate, Roh Moo-hyun, defeated the opposition candidate, Lee Hoi-chang, in the presidential election held in December 2002. Many aspects of Roh's victory over Lee, however, made subsequent governing difficult. First, it was one of the closest contests in the history of Korea. Roh received 48.91 percent of the total votes cast, while Lee received 46.59 percent, with the remaining 4.5 percent going to minor party candidates. This difference amounts to 570,000 votes out of over 24.5 million votes cast. This small margin of victory made it more difficult for the losing side to accept the election result (much like in the U.S. presidential election of 2000).

Second, the election outcome was considered to be a stunning upset. The opposition Grand National Party (GNP) candidate, Lee Hoi-chang, had already run for the presidency against Kim Dae-jung in 1997, an election which he narrowly lost. Since then, Lee had "managed" the party with the primary goal of taking another crack at the presidency in 2002. A succession of well-timed events led to the nomination of Roh Moo-hyun, a relative lightweight even in his own party, as the governing party candidate. Prior to the scheduled presidential election in 2002, public opinion polls had consistently shown Roh Moo-hyun trailing Lee Hoi-chang (*Joongang Ilbo,* various dates, 2002). It was not until a few days before the election that the tide of public opinion began to turn. Roh's come-from-behind win in a matter of a few days made it a bitter pill to swallow for the losing side.

Third, this was the first national-level election in the history of Korea in which generational differences played a critical role in the election outcome—the old primarily supported Lee Hoi-chang, while the young preferred Roh Moo-hyun. This new generational cleavage can be traced back to several different roots. The first has to do with economic or the left-right ideological division. Lee Hoi-chang, with his nobleman's image and conservative stands on various issues, was supported by those who were well-to-do and who preferred stability, many of them happening to belong to the old generation. On the other hand, Roh Moo-hyun, a high school graduate without a college education, became a human rights lawyer by passing a difficult bar exam. He was the epitome of the self-made man and a champion of the weak and the poor, an image that appealed to the young generation.

The year 2002 was also a period when many South Koreans went through a transformation in their beliefs about the desirable place of South Korea between the United States and North Korea. The acquittal in U.S. military court of two American soldiers who caused the deaths of two Korean girls by accidentally running them over with a military vehicle enraged Korean citizens and led to countless candlelight vigils and violent demonstrations in front of the U.S. embassy throughout the year. The Bush administration's tough stance against North Korea as part of the "axis of evil" also added fuel to the debate over what North Korea was to South Koreans. Many Koreans believed that the Bush administration's North Korea policy not only undermined former President Kim Dae-jung's "Sunshine Policy" (engagement), but unnecessarily heightened tensions in the Korean peninsula.

Under these circumstances, the older so-called 6-25 (the Korean War) generation was quite suspicious of the real intentions of North Korea and placed greater weight on maintaining the traditional military alliance with the United States. Lee Hoi-chang had continuously stated his preferences for a North Korean aid policy based on "reciprocity" and called for the cessation of all monetary aid to the North that could be

Table 7.1. Perecentage of Votes Won (by Candidates and Age Groups), Presidential Election, 2002.

Age group	Lee Hoi-chang (Grand National Party	Roh Moo-hyun (New Millennium Democratic Party	Others
20s	31.7	62.1	6.2
30s	33.9	59.3	6.8
40s	48.7	47.4	3.9
50s+	58.3	39.8	1.9

subverted to funding its nuclear programs. Naturally, Lee was a favorite among the older, established generations in South Korea. On the other hand, Roh Moo-hyun advocated continued cooperation with the North to prevent heightened tension in the Korean peninsula. Further, he seemingly took quite a strong position toward the United States. He indicated that as president he would establish an equal relationship between the United States and Korea. His independent position was extremely popular among the younger so-called post-6-25 (or post–Korean War) generation (*Joongang Ilbo*, various dates, 2002).

Table 7.1 shows the split between the old and the young in the presidential election of 2002. As we can see, voters in their twenties and thirties overwhelmingly supported Roh Moo-hyun. On the other hand, voters in their fifties and above overwhelmingly voted for Lee Hoi-chang. Those in their forties constitute some sort of boundary between the two contending generations.

In short, we can say that the 2002 presidential election in Korea split the country into two. A progressive candidate supported by the younger generation scored a stunning come-from-behind win over the conservative candidate supported by the old and well-to-do, after which the latter felt quite bitter and were not quite willing to accept the result of the election.

Events Leading to the Impeachment Vote

Since the democratic opening in 1987, most Korean presidents have had to face divided governments with majority oppositions in the national assembly. Roh Tae-woo (not to be confused with Roh Moo-hyun), who

Table 7.2. Seat Distribution in the National Assembly, I.

Political Parties	After the 16th general election in 2000	As of January 2004
Grand National Party	133	148
New Millennium Democratic Party	115	60
United Liberal Democrats	17	10
Woori Party	n/a	47
Others	8	6
Total	273*	271**

* As stated in note 5.17, the size of the national assembly was reduced to 273 for the 2000 election by the Kim Dae-jung government.
** A death and a conviction reduced the number of assemblymen by two.

was elected in 1987, began with the governing Democratic Justice Party with a majority of seats in the assembly, which shrank to a minority party in the following election. Roh's solution was a three-party merger to create a dominant governing party in 1990 (chapter 3). Subsequently, Kim Young-sam and Kim Dae-jung, when they faced strong opposition after their elections as president, had to rely on quite undemocratic means, such as utilizing the Supreme Prosecutor's Office to tame the opposition assembly members and to induce party switching among them (chapter 5).

Roh Moo-hyun, when elected president, not only faced a majority opposition party in the GNP but a significant portion of his own party which had not supported him at the time of the nomination contest. With or without signals from the Blue House, the presidential mansion in Korea, those within the governing New Millennium Democratic Party (NMDP) who were friendly to President Roh defected from it to establish a new governing party. The result was the founding of the so-called Woori ("Our") Party in 2003.

Table 7.2 shows the seat distributions in the national assembly in Korea. The middle column shows the seat distribution among political parties after the national assembly elections in 2000. The far right column shows the seat distribution as of January 2004, after the founding of the Woori Party. Even after the establishment of the de facto governing Woori Party, the Roh government's base was quite weak within the national assembly. Further, Roh supporters' defection from the NMDP in the end turned it into a hostile opposition, since its remaining members felt betrayed by the Roh supporters.

Throughout 2003 and early 2004, Korean society was swept by revelations of many wrongdoings on the part of politicians and big business involving illegal donation/collection and spending of campaign contributions at the time of the 2002 presidential election. With skyrocketing public anger, in January 2004 thirteen national assemblymen were arrested and charged with various corruption practices involving mishandling of money. The Supreme Prosecutor's Office indicated that more national assemblypersons were under investigation. With most of those under arrest or investigation being GNP and NMDP members, they felt that they were being unfairly targeted by the Supreme Prosecutor's Office, which was, at least in theory, part of the executive branch under the head of state, the president.

In a press conference in early 2004, President Roh stated that he hoped the governing Woori Party would acquire as many seats as possible in the upcoming national assembly elections scheduled in April. This remark enraged the opposition, since under the Korean election law, public officials are prohibited from openly supporting a particular political party (although the law itself sounds pretty unrealistic). The National Election Commission formally warned the president against further similar remarks. Now the opposition demanded a public apology by the president for the remark. Otherwise, according to the opposition, they would push for the impeachment of President Roh, as the GNP and the NMDP combined had more than the two-thirds supermajority in the national assembly necessary to pass the impeachment motion. According to the opposition, there were three reasons for potential impeachment of President Roh: (1) violation of the election law through his public support of the Woori Party, (2) financial wrongdoings of Roh's relatives and close supporters, and (3) economic mismanagement resulting in a near crisis situation during the first year of the Roh regime.

In a nationally televised press interview in March, President Roh refused to apologize in relation to the violation of election law. This further enraged the opposition assemblymen, and many who had been reluctant to support his impeachment were now leaning toward voting for it. On March 12, the historic vote was taken. The governing Woori Party assemblymen, lacking the necessary one-third of the votes to block the impeachment, occupied the assembly president's podium to prevent the vote itself, but were dragged out of the chamber by assembly security. In a subsequent vote cast by the opposition only, 193 out of 195 voted for the impeachment, exceeding the necessary two-thirds majority (181) by twelve votes. As a result, the president was impeached. The case was then sent to the Constitutional Court for a final decision.[1] Roh's presidential powers were immediately suspended, and Prime Minister Koh Gun became the acting head of state (*Hankuk Ilbo,* various dates, 2004).

The Impeachment Game

Why did President Roh refuse to accept the opposition's demand for an apology and take the risk of impeachment, knowing the opposition had a sufficient number of votes? Also, why did the opposition go ahead and impeach the president at the risk of punishment by the electorate, with the national assembly elections only a month away? These are puzzling questions, since neither side seemed to have acted in a rational fashion. This situation is further complicated since neither side knew with certainty whether the Constitutional Court would uphold or overturn the impeachment and how the electorate would react to the vote. Bayesian game theory offers tools capable of analyzing situations where at least one player is uncertain about part of the extensive form (Gibbons 1992; Morrow 1994). In this section, I attempt to answer the puzzling questions posed above by building a Bayesian game-theoretic model in which both the president and the opposition face the uncertainties described above.

This situation is depicted in an extensive form in figure 7.1. In this game, Nature goes first and determines the type of electorate between one that punishes the opposition for the impeachment and one that does not, a decision that is not known to the president or the opposition. Further, the two players are not certain about whether or not the Constitutional Court will uphold the impeachment once the vote passes in the national assembly. Then, the president decides whether to publicly apologize (A) or not (~A) as the opposition demanded. Finally, the opposition decides whether to impeach the president (I) or not (~I). Given the amount of uncertainty involved in this game regarding the types of the electorate and the Constitutional Court, both the president and the opposition face complicated decision-making calculations, which, in turn, makes our analysis difficult. Close observation, however, allows us to simplify the extensive form in figure 7.1.

First, if the president apologizes, the opposition gets what they demanded, namely having him admit he violated the election law and

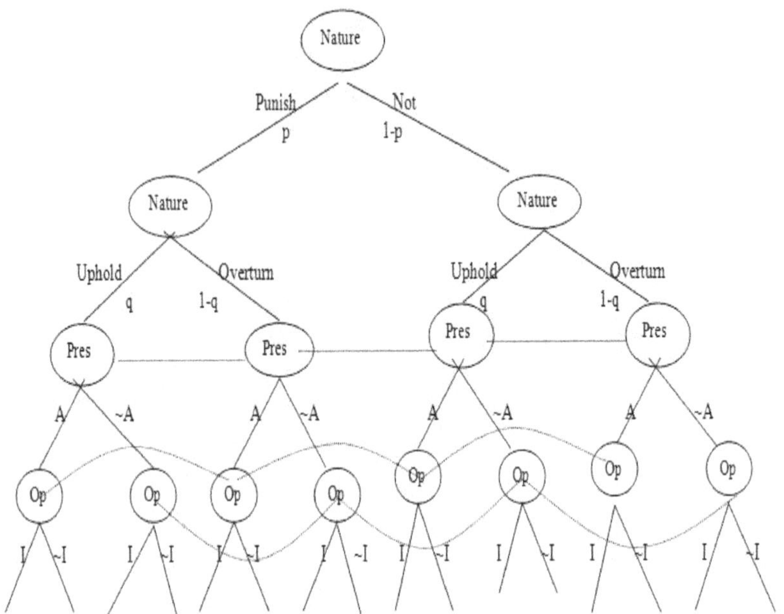

Fig. 7.1. The Impeachment game.
*The specific outcomes are omitted for lack of space.
**The dotted lines are information sets showing the amount of information available to each player. The fact that all four of the president's decision nodes are connected with a dotted line means he does not have complete information about Nature's choices. The opposition's two information sets show that it does not know Nature's choices with certainty, but does know the president's choice.

causing him to lose face. Then the opposition does not have an incentive to impeach the president at this point. Indeed, it should avoid doing so, since such an act would definitely create the impression of its being unreasonable. Thus, we can say that the opposition's "dominant action" is not to impeach once the president apologizes. So, once the president apologizes, the opposition does not have any real choice to make, and we will declare that the game is over. This will allow us to prune the extensive form in figure 7.1. This also means that when Nature chooses between "punish" and "not" in the beginning of the game, it chooses between the electorate that punishes and one that does not *when the opposition impeaches after the president decides not to apologize.*

Second, given the outcome of surveys of both governing party and opposition members by media sources, both the president (or the govern-

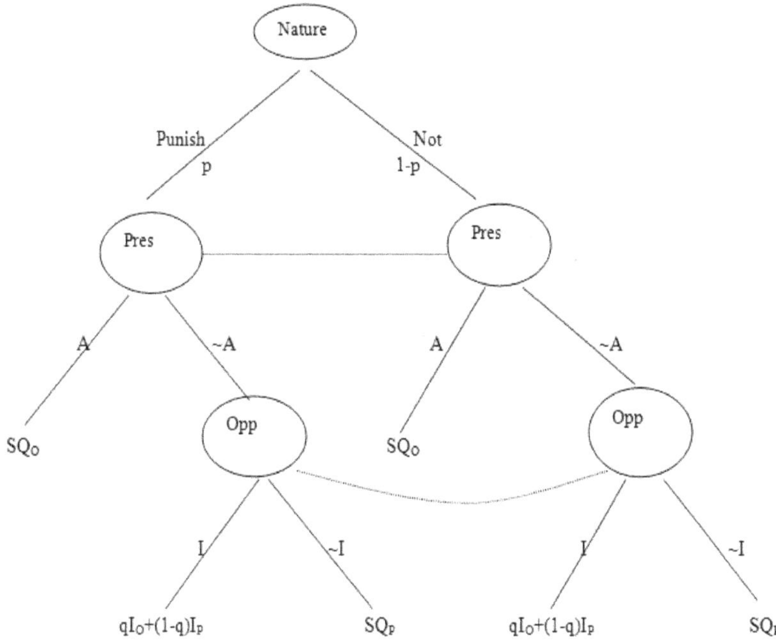

Figure 7.2. The Impeachment game: A reduced form

ing party) and the opposition seemed to have formed subjective probabilities about the Constitutional Court's decision at the time they actually made their choices. Right after the impeachment vote, a poll was taken among the assemblymen about the prospect of the impeachment being upheld by the Constitutional Court. Of the GNP assemblymen, 60.7 percent expected it to be upheld, while the number was 50 percent among the NMDP members. Given the assembly seat distribution between the two parties, the percentage of the opposition members who expected the Constitutional Court to uphold the impeachment amounted to roughly 59 percent. It is interesting to note that none of the Woori Party members expected it to happen (*Yonhap News,* March 17, 2004). Given these known subjective probabilities, I will use these numbers when I try to solve the game in figure 7.1. The two points I made above reduce the extensive form in figure 7.1 to the one in figure 7.2.

In this reduced game tree, once the president publicly apologizes, the outcome is the Status Quo—no impeachment—under the opposition terms (SQ_O). If the president does not apologize and the opposition does not impeach, then the outcome is the Status Quo under the president's terms (SQ_P). If the president does not apologize and the opposition impeaches him, then the outcome is a probability distribution over the scenarios in which the Constitutional Court upholds the impeachment (I_O) and does not (I_P). As stated earlier, both the president and the opposition had subjective assessment of the value of q. Of course, we still need to assess the impact of the two types of the electorate, the one that punishes the opposition for the impeachment and the one that does not.

Now let us look at this impeachment game from President Roh's point of view. The possible outcomes are: SQ_O when he apologizes, SQ_P when he does not apologize and the opposition does not impeach him, and $qI_O+(1-q)I_P$ when he does not apologize and the opposition impeaches him. Although, in principle, the president's utility is not affected by Nature's choice between "Punish" and "Not" (since it is the opposition that is punished if the electorate chooses to do so), it is indirectly affected by Nature's choice, since if it chooses "punish," the governing party is likely to gain seats in the assembly, given the zero-sum nature of the assembly elections. From the survey of the national assemblymen cited above and assuming that the president shared the same information with the governing party members, we can assume that the president's subjective probability of the Constitutional Court's upholding the impeachment, say q' = 0. Then $U_P[qI_O+(1-q)I_P] = U_P(I_P)$ at the time he made the decision. So, for the president, the utilities of three possible outcomes are $U_P(SQ_O)$, $U_P(SQ_P)$, and $U_P(I_P)$. Obviously, $U_P(SQ_P) > U_P(SQ_O)$, since the president would rather not apologize and admit inappropriate behavior if he can avoid impeachment. The magnitude of $U_P(I_P)$ is what interests us most, the utility to the president when the opposition impeaches him but the impeachment is overturned by the Constitutional Court. More discussion about this possibility follows below.

The situation is more complicated for the opposition. Unlike the president, the opposition must consider Nature's choice between "Punish" and "Not." Based on the survey of the national assemblymen cited above, we will assume that the opposition's subjective probability of the Constitutional Court's upholding the impeachment are, say, q" = .59. Then $U_O[qI_O+(1-q)I_P] = U_O[.59I_O + .41I_P]$. For the opposition, obviously $U_O(SQ_O) > U_O(SQ_P)$. The magnitude of $U_O[.59I_O + .41I_P]$ would depend on whether the opposition thinks the electorate will punish them (that is, vote against them) for the impeachment vote or not. Obviously, it would be the worst possible outcome if the Constitutional Court decides to overturn the impeachment and the electorate chooses to punish the opposition.

Aftermath of the Impeachment

To the opposition's amazement, the reaction to the impeachment was near-universal condemnation. Virtually all NGOs, labor organizations, student groups, scholars, and lawyers' associations denounced the vote and declared civil disobedience. Massive demonstrations ensued (*Hankuk Ilbo,* various dates, 2004).

The national assembly elections were held on April 15, as scheduled. The outcome of the elections, along with the seat distribution just before the elections, is shown in table 7.3. The elections resulted in the new assembly's composition being quite different from that of the previous one. For our purposes, we cannot overlook the demise of the opposition, especially of the NMDP, and the political victory of the governing Woori Party. The GNP also lost a significant proportion of seats, considering the increase in the total number of seats in the assembly to 299 (from 273). This was the first time in nineteen years that the governing party had acquired a simple majority of seats (which requires 150 in a 299-seat assembly) in the national assembly in Korea.

Surveys of the electorate indicated that the impeachment was the overwhelming criterion for their vote choice. In the 2004 national assem-

Table 7.3. Seat Distribution in the National Assembly, II.

Political parties	As of January 2004	After the 17th general election in 2004
Grand National Party	148	121
New Millennium Democratic Party	60	9
United Liberal Democrats	10	4
Woori Party	47	152
Democratic Labor Party	0	10
Others	6	3
Total	271	299*

* The new electoral law enacted just before the elections increased the number of seats in the national assembly back to 299.

bly elections, politics clearly was not "local." Voters paid little attention to the candidates, but looked primarily at their party labels (*Joongang Ilbo,* various dates, 2004). Obviously, the electorate did not approve of the impeachment vote by the opposition and punished it accordingly.[2]

On May 12, 2004, the nine-member Constitutional Court overturned the impeachment, by a majority vote, reinstating President Roh to office.[3] It ruled that although some minor election law violations actually occurred, they were not serious enough to warrant a presidential impeachment. This verdict was widely accepted by the Korean public. With a new political lease on life, coupled with control of the national assembly, Roh Moo-hyun was free to pursue a more activist agenda, which actually happened for the rest of his term.[4]

Assessment

Now I will assess the choices made by the president and the opposition in March of 2004.[5] As we already know, President Roh Moo-hyun chose not to apologize (~A) and the opposition chose to impeach (I). As I stated above, $U_P(SQ_P) > U_P(SQ_O)$ and $U_P[qI_O+(1-q)I_P] = U_P(I_P)$ since the governing party and the president *believed* that there was zero chance of the Constitutional Court upholding the impeachment. I_P is the outcome when the opposition impeaches him, which is overturned by the Constitutional Court. Yes, the president's authority might be undermined if he should be impeached even if it is overturned by the Constitutional Court. But was it necessarily a terrible outcome compared to SQ_O, the outcome in which he publicly acknowledges that he has violated the law and apologizes for it? In this case, not only is his authority damaged, but there would be zero chance of helping the governing Woori Party in the upcoming elections. In the case of I_P, at least the president may be able to *induce* sympathy on the part of the electorate and the resulting punishment of the opposition. Then, when the president chose between A and ~A in March 2004, the choice was in fact between (1) certain public humiliation with little chance of enhancing governability (SQ_O) and (2) some sort of lottery between complete vindication (SQ_P) and the impeachment being overturned by the Constitutional Court, which might actually enhance the power of the governing party through the weakening of the opposition. In short, choosing confrontation (~A, choosing not to apologize) might not have looked so bad, given the choices he had.

Now let us move over to the opposition's choice. Once the president decided not to apologize, the opposition was left with going ahead and impeaching him or backing away from its initial threat of impeachment. As we found out above, the opposition *believed* that there was nearly a 60 percent chance of the Constitutional Court upholding the impeachment. Then the opposition's choice was between a good chance of driving President Roh out of office, probably its most preferred outcome, and a complete vindication of the president (and the opposition's loss of face and credibility). Even so, the opposition's choice of impeachment makes sense only if it *believed* that the chance of the electorate's adverse reaction (punishment) was not that high. Although I do not have information to directly support this claim, given the split of society between the governing party and the opposition supporters following the presidential election of 2002 and subsequent political developments, the opposition probably had every reason to believe that at least its core constituents, nearly half of the population, would stay with it, which apparently didn't happen.

In sum, despite the seemingly erratic behavior on both sides, the president and the opposition played the impeachment game in a rational fashion, *given their preferences, the choices they had, and the information they had (their beliefs) about the state of Nature* (Ordeshook 1986). The difference was in the accuracy of the information they held. Looking at subsequent developments, President Roh and the governing Woori Party had accurate information or beliefs about the Constitutional Court's likely decision and the nature of the electorate. It was the opposition that had completely misread the potential reactions of both the Constitutional Court and the electorate. And that made a critical difference in the final outcome of the impeachment game in Korea.

Conclusion

On March 12, 2004, a stunning political event happened in Korea. Its national assembly impeached President Roh Moo-hyun only a year into his term as president. The opposition parties, with over two-thirds of the seats in the assembly, decided to use their numerical strength only one month before the next national assembly elections. It is troublesome since the impeachment of President Roh appears to have been the result of a set of irrational decisions. The investigation of actual events above reveal the preferences, choices, and the information about the nature of the political situation the president and the opposition held at the time they made their decisions. Based on this information and utilizing a game-theoretic model, I have shown that the choices made by both sides were indeed not that surprising or irrational.

As stated in chapter 1, there is an on-going debate about the usefulness of rational choice theory in analyzing particular real-world events. Critics argue that it is preoccupied with theory development, accompanied by a striking "paucity of empirical application" (Green and Ian Shapiro 1994). This chapter adds another case to the list of real-world events that have been successfully explained using rational choice approach.

8

Concluding Remarks

South Korea has been looked at as one of the countries to have gone through the process of democratic transition most successfully after a rapid economic development (apart from occasional scuffles among the members of the national assembly that we see on CNN).[1] I have shown in this book that the process of democratic transition in Korea since 1987 has been more or less "big-event" oriented. Political leaders have played important roles in those big events, though not necessarily in the pursuit of some normative democratic ideal as much as in an effort to protect and further their own political interests. Even so, the outcome has been a pretty successful democratic transition! Let me briefly add political developments in Korea since Roh Moo-hyun's impeachment and reinstatement in 2004.

Latest Political Developments in Korea

As I mentioned in chapter 6, there was little uncertainty about South Korea's preferences in its conciliatory policies toward North Korea in the late 1990s and early 2000s, as both the Kim Dae-jung and Roh Moo-hyun governments openly pursued reconciliation policies. However, after five tumultuous years of Roh Moo-hyun's rule (see below), this situation changed when the opposition Grand National Party candidate, Lee Myung-bak, was elected president in late 2007.

The opposition had been quite critical of the Kim and Roh governments' reconciliation policies and had promised to take a more conservative (frequently called "reciprocal") approach toward the North. Lee's victory created uncertainty as to what path the new South Korean government would take regarding cooperation with the North.

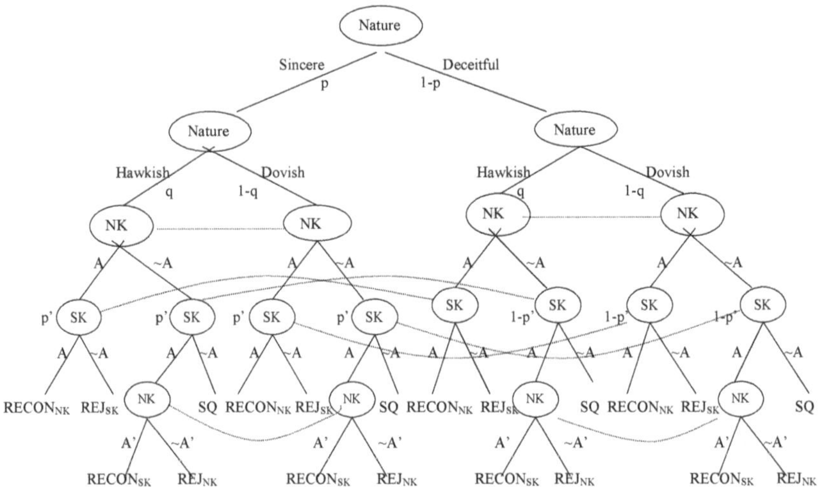

Figure 8.1. A potential South Korea–North Korea Bayesian game under the Lee Myung-bak government.

This meant that neither side would be certain about the other's intentions in the interaction between North and South Korea, a situation represented in the extensive form in figure 8.1. As before, there would be two possible types of North Korean leadership picked by Nature, a sincere one and a deceitful one. Further, now there would be two possible types of South Korean leadership, which might be called hawkish and dovish. In short, the strategic interaction between the two Koreas became more complicated after the election of a more conservative government.

On the other hand, in the United States then-candidate Barack Obama promised to sit down with anyone—friends and enemies alike, without any preconditions—to pursue peaceful resolutions of conflicts, a rather dramatic change from the previous Bush administration. What this means is that the U.S.-North Korea interaction could be less complicated than before, and follow the pattern in figure 6.1 rather than the one in figure 6.2.

It appears that the electorates of the two ally nations, the United States and South Korea, produced two conflicting types of governments as far as their attitudes toward North Korea are concerned—that is, the Kim/Roh-Bush pairs and the Lee-Obama pair. Due to the simultaneous nature of the North Korea–South Korea game and the U.S.-North Korea game that

I pointed out in chapter 6, these conflicting combinations cause the interpretation of North Korean behavior to be more difficult.

Since its inauguration, the Obama administration seems to have been overwhelmed by so many issues and crises, both domestic and international: the worldwide financial crisis, the universal healthcare debate, the British Petroleum oil leak, difficult situations in Iraq, Iran, Afghanistan, Pakistan, and the Middle East, among others. This has made the North Korea issue a low-priority one, which seems to have made the North Korean leadership rather impatient. A prolonged delay in dealing with the North, coupled with uncertainty created by the advent of the conservative Lee Myung-bak government in South Korea, may cause the North to choose a perilous course of action. We recently have witnessed the North Korean torpedoing of a South Korean naval vessel and shelling of a South Korean island near the border with North Korea in 2010, which caused significant military and civilian fatalities. Some North Korea specialists find the causes of these North Korean actions in its domestic political situation—that is, the on-going succession process from Kim Jong-il to his son, Kim Jong-eun. However, we can also view them as a desperate, attention-grabbing behavior on the part of its government to make the North Korea issue a high priority one again.

I analyzed the decisions involving the impeachment of President Roh Moo-hyun in chapter 7. As noted, he was reinstated, served out his term, and retired from politics in 2008. Soon after leaving the presidency, though, a bribery scandal involving some of his family members was uncovered. The family members and the former president himself were placed under investigation by the Supreme Prosecutor's Office.

This was a shock to many in Korea, because the whole premise of Roh's presidency was transparency and clean politics, which for many compensated for his unrefined behavior. At the height of the investigation in May 2009, the former president committed suicide by jumping off a cliff behind his retirement home. This incident divided the Korean population over the issue of whether the prosecutors were fair in their investigation or were acting as agents of the new conservative government.

In July 2009, former president Kim Dae-jung was hospitalized for pneumonia, and his health was failing rather quickly. He then lost consciousness and was put on life support. Many politicians visited his hospital bed and wished him a speedy recovery. After his visit to Kim Dae-jung's deathbed in August, Kim Young-sam declared that the rivalry between the two Kims had ended and that the two had completely reconciled whatever differences they had had (*Yonhap News,* August 10, 2009). It was, however, a rather hollow reconciliation, because one of them had been unconscious. As I have shown above, the two Kims' *personal rivalry* had a great impact on the direction and the pace of democratic transition in Korea. Kim Dae-jung died a few days later. He will be remembered for his efforts to open the door to the North; but precisely because of these efforts, his presidency will be evaluated according to how the relationship with the North progresses in the future.

In late 2009, Korean political leaders started discussing potential constitutional change. There is a widespread perception that Korean presidents are vulnerable to corruption since power is concentrated in their hands. Also, regionalism is still strong. There seems to be agreement among political leaders that the president's tenure should be changed from a single five-year term to a pair of four-year terms, so that the incumbent president must face reelection, which will enhance accountability. They are also looking into changing electoral institutions to lessen the degree of regional division, an exercise that Korean legislators went through during the Kim Dae-jung presidency as well (see chapter 5 above).

The constitutional revision must be initiated by the national assembly in Korea. One thing we are certain of is that the self-interested politicians will not try any new system that will heavily damage their vested interest in the status quo. For example, although many recognize that proportional representation would provide more fair representation as far as the regions are concerned, we must not expect the political leaders to accept the abolition or a drastic reduction in single-member districts. If faced with strong public opinion demanding regionally fair representation, they may turn to a compromise solution of multimember district electoral institutions without completely accepting proportional representation. Whatever turns out to be the outcome of the current debate, the ultimate goal of fair, corruption-free representation will depend to a large degree on how political parties choose candidates (or whether they adopt open or closed lists in the case of proportional representation). Obviously, the leader-centered and paternalistic nature of Korean parties, which made the application of the rational choice approach easier in my analyses in this book, is not a good ingredient for democratic politics.

Returning to the Main Point

Some scholars have doubted the applicability of rational choice theory in developing nations because actors' goals and preferences depend on culturally unique values and there is no way to characterize people's goals and preferences independent of culture (Geertz 1971). In this book, I have tried to show that, despite cultural differences, common goals and preferences may be assumed in analyses of political events across countries. More specifically, politicians' desire for greater power and concern for physical security and welfare are cross-cultural and nearly universal. Once we recognize the elements of a core set of human interests, we begin to see regularities in developing nations that can be meaningfully analyzed with the concept of rationality.

The importance of group identity and the adherence to collective norms are often emphasized in analyses of traditional (especially Asian) societies (Polanyi 1957; Cheng and Tallian 1995). In my analysis of the three-party merger in chapter 3, the fact that almost all members of the three parties joined the potentially controversial merger might be seen as devotion to a collectivity (party) and loyalty to the leader. However, a thorough look at the political circumstances dictating their behavior reveals that they more likely were trying to maximize (or protect) their self-interest. Perhaps more often than we realize, what appears to be the pursuit of a collective norm may be the pursuit of self-interest, and group identity can sometimes be formed as a result of the aggregation of individual self-interest.

Therefore, it is important in any rational choice analysis to define carefully the goals of each player and his or her preferences for possible outcomes. In short, what is important is what goes into each player's utility function (Frank 1990). For example, for the three-party merger analyzed in chapter 3, Kim Young-sam and Kim Dae-jung wanted to assume power; Roh Tae-woo wanted to guarantee his future security and prolong his party's rule. Because of the leader-centered and paternalistic nature of Korean political parties, party members saw it to be in their interest to side with their leaders. All the actors pursued their preferred outcome rationally. The result was the Democratic Liberal Party.

Therefore, what is necessary in any rational choice analysis of real-world events is area expertise, because the acceptable set of participants, strategies, and preferences can only be determined within the confines of the particular culture in which the events in question are played out. In the end, what this book suggests is a marriage of rational choice theory and area studies, rather than "the rational choice vs. area studies controversy."

Appendix A

Solution for the Equilibrium of the South-North Bayesian Game

The equilibrium of the North Korea–South Korea Bayesian game will be solved in appendix A. The most commonly used solution concept for dynamic Bayesian games is Perfect Bayesian Equilibrium (PBE), which I adopt here. First of all, it is easy to see that North Korea has a dominant action on its last move. The sincere type will always choose A' while the deceitful type will choose ~A'. Now I focus our attention on North Korea's first move.

[1] AA (pooling on A)

U_{SK} (A) = p U_{SK}(RECON) + (1-p) U_{SK}(EXP_N)
U_{SK} (~A) = U_{SK}(REJ_S)

If SK's best response to NK's choice of AA is ~A, then NK has the incentive to switch to ~A. Therefore, the PBE does not include SK's choice of ~A. If SK's best response to NK's choice of AA is A, then both types of NK get the best possible outcomes and do not have the incentive to switch. This is true when U_{SK} (A) ≥ U_{SK} (~A). This inequality condition is satisfied when p ≥ [U_{SK}(REJ_S) - U_{SK}(EXP_N)] / [U_{SK}(RECON) - U_{SK}(EXP_N)].

Therefore, a PBE is: {(A/A', A/~A'), A, p ≥ [U_{SK}(REJ_S) - U_{SK}(EXP_N)] / [U_{SK}(RECON) - U_{SK}(EXP_N)]}.

[2] A~A (separating with the sincere type choosing A)

p' = 1. SK's best response is A, and it receives U_{SK}(RECON) or

U_{SK}(SQ) depending on NK's type. A~A is the equilibrium strategy for NK only if SK's best response to NK's choice of A is ~A. This is incompatible with p' = 1. So, there is no PBE under this scenario.

[3] ~AA (separating with the sincere type choosing ~A)

p' = 0. In response to SK's best response, (~A), NK has the incentive to change its current strategy. Therefore, there is no PBE under this scenario.

[4] ~A~A (pooling on ~A)

SK's information set is off the equilibrium path. For ~A~A to be part of the equilibrium profile, SK's best response to NK's deviation must be ~A (that is, $U_{SK}(A) \leq U_{SK}(\sim A)$). This is the case when $p \leq [U_{SK}(REJ_S) - U_{SK}(EXP_N)] / [U_{SK}(RECON) - U_{SK}(EXP_N)]$.

Therefore, a PBE is: {(~A/A', ~A/~A'), ~A, $p \leq [U_{SK}(REJ_S) - U_{SK}(EXP_N)] / [U_{SK}(RECON) - U_{SK}(EXP_N)]$}.

The details of the equilibrium solution above lead to the following observations:

Observation 1: All PBEs in the North–South-Korea game are pooling equilibria.

From [1] and [4] above.

Observation 2: SK should pursue A only when p is high.

From [1] above.

Observation 3: The PBE under the first pooling equilibrium is more efficient for NK than the one under the second. This means that both types of NK will try to convince SK that p is high.

From [1] and [4] above.

Appendix B

Solution for the Equilibrium of the U.S.–North Korea Bayesian Game

The equilibrium of the U.S.–North Korea Bayesian game is solved here. Again, I use the notion of Perfect Bayesian Equilibrium (PBE). First of all, it is easy to see that North Korea has a dominant action on its last move. The sincere type will always choose A' while the deceitful type will choose ~A'. Now I narrow our attention down to North Korea's first move.

[1] AA (pooling on A)

When NK is pooling on A, the U.S. equilibrium strategy is ~AA~AA. Since at least the deceitful NK always has an incentive to switch, there is no PBE under this scenario.

[2] A~A (separating with the sincere type choosing A)

When the U.S. observes NK's choice of A, then p' = 1 and the U.S.'s best response is ~AA. When the U.S. observes NK's choice of ~A, then p' = 0 and the US's best response is ~A~A. The deceitful NK does not have incentive to switch. For sincere NK, $U_{NK}(A) = qU_{NK}(REJ_{US}) + (1\text{-}q) U_{NK}(RECON_{NK})$ and $U_{NK}(\sim A) = qU_{NK}(SQ) + (1\text{-}q)U_{NK}(RECON_{US})$. For sincere NK not to have incentive to switch from its equilibrium strategy, $U_{NK}(A) \geq U_{NK}(\sim A)$ must hold. It is true when $q \geq [U_{NK}(RECON_{US}) - U_{NK}(RECON_{NK})] / [U_{NK}(RECON_{US}) + U_{NK}(REJ_{US}) - U_{NK}(RECON_{NK}) - U_{NK}(SQ)]$.

Therefore a PBE is: {(A/A'~A/~A'), (~AA~A~A), $q \geq [U_{NK}(RECON_{US})$

- $U_{NK}(RECON_{NK})] / [U_{NK}(RECON_{US}) + U_{NK}(REJ_{US}) - U_{NK}(RECON_{NK}) - U_{NK}(SQ)]\}$.

[3] ~AA (separating with the sincere type choosing ~A)

When the U.S. observes NK's choice of A, then p' = 0 and the U.S.'s best response is ~AA. When the U.S. observes NK's choice of ~A, then p' = 1 and the U.S.'s best response is ~A~A. Since at least the deceitful NK always has an incentive to switch its action, there is no PBE under this scenario.

[4] ~A~A (pooling on ~A)

The hawkish U.S.'s best response is ~A. For the dovish U.S., its best response is A if $p' \geq [U_{US}(SQ) - U_{US}(REJ_{NK})] / [U_{US}(RECON_{US}) - U_{US}(REJ_{NK})]$. Otherwise, it is ~A. The deceitful NK does not have an incentive to switch. If the dovish U.S.'s equilibrium action is A, then the sincere NK does not have an incentive to switch, either.

Therefore a PBE is $\{(\sim A/A'\sim A/\sim A'), (\sim AA\sim AA), p' \geq [U_{US}(SQ) - U_{US}(REJ_{NK})] / [U_{US}(RECON_{US}) - U_{US}(REJ_{NK})], q\}$.

If, on the other hand, the dovish U.S. responds with ~A ($p' < [U_{US}(SQ) - U_{US}(REJ_{NK})] / [U_{US}(RECON_{US}) - U_{US}(REJ_{NK})]$), the sincere NK has incentive to switch to A if $U_{NK}(A) \geq U_{NK}(\sim A)$. To prevent this, $U_{NK}(\sim A) \geq U_{NK}(A)$ must hold for the sincere NK. This is true when $q \geq [U_{NK}(RECON_{NK}) - U_{NK}(SQ)] / [U_{NK}(RECON_{NK}) - U_{NK}(REJ_{US})]$.

Therefore, another PBE is $\{(\sim A/A'\sim A/\sim A'), (\sim A\sim A\sim A\sim A), p' < [U_{US}(SQ) - U_{US}(REJ_{NK})] / [U_{US}(RECON_{US}) - U_{US}(REJ_{NK})], q \geq [U_{NK}(RECON_{NK}) - U_{NK}(SQ)] / [U_{NK}(RECON_{NK}) - U_{NK}(REJ_{US})]\}$.

The equilibrium solution above leads to the following observations:

Observation 4: The hawkish US's equilibrium strategy does not depend on NK's type.

Simple backward induction shows that the hawkish U.S.'s optimal strategy is always ~A regardless of NK's type.

Observation 5: The dovish U.S. will always reciprocate the accommodation initiated by NK. Whether the dovish U.S. will initiate accommodation in the absence of NK's initial accommodation will depend on the value of p'.

Observation 6: The deceitful NK never initiates A.

This comes from the three PBEs under [2] and [4] above.

Observation 7: Long-term reconciliation is possible if NK is sincere and the U.S. is dovish.

Among the three PBEs above, only the combination of a sincere NK and a dovish U.S. leads to RECON outcomes.

Observation 8: The combination of a deceitful NK and a hawkish U.S. always leads to SQ.

From the three PBEs above.

Notes

1. Rational Choice, Area Expertise, and Democratic Transition in Developing Societies

1. For a concise summary of criticisms of rational choice approaches to the third world, see Little (1991).

2. Of course, the role of political elites has already been studied extensively in the context of political development and democratization (e.g., Dahl 1971; Huntington 1984; Przeworski 1992; Rustow 1970; Valenzuela 1992; O'Donnell and Schmitter 1986; and Burton, Gunther, and Higley 1992, just to name a few).

3. I do not claim that this is the first set of good rational-choice applications to real-world events. By now there are many, including early applications, such as Popkin 1979; Bates 1981; Bates 1988; Bates 1989; and Geddes 1991.

2. Kims' Dilemma and the Politics of Rivalry

1. For the historical background in this section, I am heavily indebted to Han Sung-joo (1990), Kihl (1988), Sohn (1989), and "The Agitating 80s," a special series by the Munhwa Broadcasting Company (1990).

2. Kihl 1988, 20–21. In February of 1986, the Haitian dictator, Jean-Claude Duvalier, went into exile while the Portuguese president was elected by the general public for the first time in sixty years. In the same month, Marcos was ousted and Corazon Aquino was sworn in as the president of the Philippines. In 1987, the Soviet Communist Party adopted secret voting while the Taiwanese government lifted the thirty-eight-year-old martial law.

3. Although it is a very plausible one, given the two Kims' past histories (which affects their subsequent preferences), Assumption 1 is not necessary for the argument I make in this chapter. It is adopted here mainly for simplicity of illustration.

4. The construction of Equations 1, 2, and 3 is not an attempt to assign exact numerical values to these equations and, thus, the outcomes they represent. These equations should be seen as heuristic devices that help us to establish Kim1's ordinal preference between the (Stay, Stay) outcome and the (Resign, Stay) outcome. That is, they make it easier to make a reasonable conclusion about which outcome was preferred by each Kim. We are not interested in, and cannot determine, how much one outcome was preferred to the other.

5. For details of this strategy, see *International Herald Tribune,* November 11, 1987, and Lee Young-suk (1992). The information on the distribution of eligible voters was borrowed from Kihl (1988, 17).

6. Since the three events of Kim1 winning, Kim2 winning, and Roh winning were collectively exhaustible (there were only three realistically possible outcomes of the 1987 presidential election), $P_{ss/1}$, $P_{ss/2}$, and $P_{ss/3}$ should sum up to 1. Therefore, each Kim's assigning high value to $P_{ss/1}$ (assessing his own chance of winning as being very high) means very low values for $P_{ss/2}$ and $P_{ss/3}$.

7. The details about the process and the outcome of the voting at the national convention of the New Democratic Party in 1970 came from Gang-shik Lee (1970) and Sang-woo Lee (1992). Kim Dae-jung went ahead and made an impressive showing against the incumbent president, Park Chung-hee, in the presidential election of April 1971. He received 43.6 percent of the total votes cast, against Park's 51.2 percent. President Park's majority, allowing for regional factors, was a mere 0.2 percent of the total votes cast, even with all the money and administrative power he mobilized. It is widely believed that Kim Dae-jung's strong showing against President Park contributed to Park's decision to abandon the direct presidential election altogether, a tradition inherited by Chun Doo-hwan. For an excellent analysis of the 1971 presidential election (and the history of authoritarian rule in Korea), see Sohn (1989, 30–45).

8. In the election of 1987, there were no provinces where Kim Dae-jung received more than 13 percent of the total votes cast, outside of Cholla provinces and the Seoul-Kyonggi region, where he was particularly strong. As a result, he finished last among the three primary candidates in all the provinces except his native Cholla provinces and the capital city of Seoul.

3. Building a New Party System

1. For Korea's new electoral system, see Brady and Mo (1992) and Cheng and Tallian (1995).

2. Han Dong-yun 1990, 168–169. Regionalism has been a dominant social cleavage in Korea since Park Chung-hee came to power in a military coup in 1961. Under Park's rule, most important investments in industry and infrastructure were concentrated around Seoul and in the Kyungsang provinces, where Park and many of his followers came from. The Kyungsang provinces were also favorably treated in elite recruitment and dominated the central government. A gap in political power and economic well-being emerged between Kyungsang provinces and the rest of the country outside of Seoul. Worst treated by the Park government were the two Cholla provinces, which produced many prominent opposition figures, including Kim Dae-jung. Park's neglect of Cholla provinces led to the impoverishment of the region at the time the country was experiencing the "economic miracle," which in turn raised a sense of bitterness and relative deprivation in Cholla. This pattern of regional discrimination and cleavage con-

tinued after the assassination of Park in 1979; Park's successors, Chun Doo-hwan and Roh Tae-woo, also came from Kyungsang provinces. The cohesion in elite cooperation and voter support in Kyungsang provinces began to decline with the emergence of the RDP, led by Kim Young-sam, who came from South Kyungsang province. Most voters in North Kyungsang, the home of Park Chung-hee, Chun Doo-hwan, and Roh Tae-woo, still supported the governing DJP, while those in the South Kyungsang province began to turn to the opposition RDP. Voters in the central region of Choongchung provinces were generally progovernment during Park's rule, since Park's second hand, Kim Jong-pil, came from this region and it was relatively well treated. However, Chun Doo-hwan ostracized Kim Jong-pil, who then established the NDRP. Voters in Choongchung provinces began to develop their own regional identity around the NDRP. In recent decades regionalism has been the most reliable predictor of voter choice in Korean elections.

3. *Dong-a Ilbo*; *Sisa Journal*; also, Ahn Gyung-hwan, "Comments on Korean Domestic Politics," *Wolgan Chosun* (December 1990): 124–136; Han Dong-yun 1990.

4. See Ahn (1995) for an assessment of the DJP strategy during the coalition bargaining. The Japanese Liberal Democratic Party split in June 1993, more than three years after Korean political leaders contemplated the merger of their parties.

5. Lee Gang-shik, "The Beginning and the End of the Presidential Candidate Nominating Convention of the New Democratic Party" [in Korean], *Shin Dong-a* (November 1970): 84–93. On the 1971 presidential election (and the history of authoritarian rule in Korea), see Sohn (1989, 30–45).

6. The location of the parties in figure 3.1 reflects in a crude manner the information about the political relationship among the leaders of the four parties. Because Kim Young-sam and Kim Dae-jung were politically least compatible, the RDP and the PPD have been put in extreme columns. Kim Jong-pil's close ties with Kim Young-sam place the NDRP next to the RDP. Roh Tae-woo's amenability to the other three puts the DJP between the PPD and the NDRP.

7. Politicians as rational actors should also evaluate the potential cost of their actions. One cost of the merger was citizen reaction to (or punishment for) the merger in the next national assembly and presidential elections. The expected cost of the merger was low due to two years of economic slowdown and political instability prior to the merger, as well as the stable political system the merger seemed to deliver (a two-party system with a dominant governing part). See chapter 4.

4. A Theory of Government-Driven Democratization

1. Only fifty-four RDP members joined the new Democratic Liberal Party, since five members of the RDP, citing the purity of the opposition, decided not

to follow suit (see table 3.1). The number of seats controlled by the new DLP increased to 217 when two independents decided to join the party later in 1990.

5. Party Preferences and Institutional Choices

1. Korea has a presidential form of government. So, when I use the term "NCNP-ULD coalition," or the "governing coalition," I do not mean the *coalition government* typical in the parliamentary system. Rather, I mean a sort of loose and power-sharing governing block based on a pre-presidential election agreement. Kim Dae-jung's governing block did not have a majority of seats in the national assembly. Under the Korean constitution, the presidential appointment of the prime minister requires the ratification of the national assembly.

2. The ULD had consistently advocated a parliamentary system as the appropriate form of government in Korea. The NCNP reversed its previous position and agreed to a constitutional change in an attempt to acquire the ULD's support in the 1997 presidential election. The GNP's former presidential candidate and other factional leaders expressed conflicting views on this issue. The party as a whole, however, seemed to be keeping its options open. The proper form of government had never been a serious issue within the GNP, and it could have gone either way depending on its political calculations. I believe it would have opposed the NCNP's position, whichever system the latter chose. Had the NCNP chosen to honor the agreement with the ULD and pushed for a constitutional change, the GNP would have declared itself a *protector* of the constitution. The GNP's flexibility on this issue forced the NCNP to prepare for two different contingencies depending upon which way it wanted to go on the constitutional issue.

3. This system has been adopted by many European countries, including Austria, Belgium, Denmark, Norway, and Sweden.

4. Korea had already experimented with a double-member district system during the Fourth Republic (1972–1980) and the Fifth Republic (1980–1987).

5. Albania, Armenia, Croatia, Georgia, Hungary, Italy, Japan, Lithuania, Macedonia, New Zealand, Russia, and Ukraine use some sort of mixed system with various PR/SMD ratios for the election of their assemblies.

6. As the negotiation with the ULD about electoral reform progressed in 1999, the NCNP's positions on the size of the national assembly and the PR/SMD ratio fluctuated (*Joongang Ilbo* May 26, 1999).

7. For whatever reason, electoral systems with an ordinal ballot structure with transferable votes (as are used in Ireland, the Australian Senate, and Malta) have never been seriously considered by any Korean political actors or scholars.

8. Israel, Moldova, Monaco, Netherlands, and Peru adopted this system for their assembly elections.

9. Of course, this is the system adopted in countries such as the United States, the United Kingdom, Canada, and New Zealand (up until its own electoral system change).

10. The Korean electoral system included predominantly SMDs with a small number of at-large (that is, proportional) seats, where the latter was determined by the number of seats each party acquired in the former.

11. There are obvious limitations in this approach, since it assumes that voter support/preferences of parties/candidates is fixed across elections, at least for the short term, when in fact it could be fluid. The NCNP would enter the next national assembly election as a governing party. First of all, good (or poor) performance in office may make a difference in the level of support for the governing party. By appearing to be equitable and competent in the face of the economic challenges, the NCNP might be able to win more votes at the margin. Second, there is such a thing as incumbent advantage, which in Korea is commonly called the governing party premium. The business community is more prone to contribute to, and the local bureaucrats are more willing to work with, the governing party at election time. The problem here, of course, is that the impact of good performance on election outcomes or the governing party's electoral advantage is not readily measurable in a nonarbitrary fashion. I do not try to incorporate these factors in the following analysis since any attempt to do so would more likely introduce arbitrariness and nonrandom measurement error. I caution readers, therefore, that the analysis in this chapter presents an informed conjecture, as most empirical studies do, with the best, readily available information.

12. The subsequent election outcomes support this assumption that the pattern of electoral support changes only gradually.

13. There are several existing seat allocation rules (known as translation formulae) that translate the PR votes into the PR seats. They include the "largest remainder" method (which was used in the Italian House of Deputies until 1993), the D'Hondt (the "highest average") method (used in Austria, Belgium, Finland, and the Italian Senate until 1993), and the Sainte-Laguë formula (used in Sweden and Norway). In the absence of any mention of seat allocation rules by political groups that advocate the PR system or a mixed system in Korea, I use the simplest and most intuitive method of translating the PR votes into seats, which assumes perfect proportionality—in each district, the PR seats are assigned in perfect proportion to the PR votes in that district, after rounding fractions, for all three electoral institutions examined in this section.

14. These districts correspond to the current administrative regions of the country. They are: the capital city of Seoul; the South Kyongsang province, including the cities of Pusan and Woolsan; the North Kyongsang province, including the city of Taegu; the Gyonggi province, including the city of Inchon; the Cholla and Jeju provinces, including the city of Kwangju; the Gangwon and Choongchung provinces, including the city of Daejon.

15. This situation changed in 1999. See the last section of this chapter for details.

16. In the 1996 National Assembly elections, for example, the NCNP received 63.7, 71, and 86.2 percent of the total votes cast, respectively, in the

two Cholla provinces and the city of Kwangju, located in Cholla. This performance allowed the party to carry thirty-six out of thirty-seven elective seats in the Cholla-Kwangju region. This has been a consistent pattern in the past, which produced a legend that nomination by the NCNP (or the Party for Peace and Democracy previously) assured election in this region. In the same election, the NCNP received 35.2, 29.5, and 27.4 percent of the total votes cast respectively in Seoul, Gyonggi, and Inchon in the capital region. With this performance, the party carried thirty out of ninety-six elective seats in the region. The most votes received by the NCNP outside of these two regions were 11.4 percent in the city of Daejon, and the party recorded a single-digit performance everywhere else. The NCNP failed to acquire a single elective seat in nine provinces and specially administered cities outside of the two regions of the party's stronghold discussed above. The party's extreme regional nature, as indicated in the election results above, has been consistent in the past.

17. It is widely known that many of the GNP assemblymen who changed their party affiliation had been under some kind of investigation, with charges varying from corruption to campaign finance violations. Interestingly enough, in many instances, investigations stopped, charges were dropped, or sentences were reduced once they switched parties. This produced what journalists sarcastically call the *yeodang mujue yadang yujue* (governing party, innocent; opposition, guilty) phenomenon (*Joongang Ilbo,* September 5, September 18, 1998). In the survey of the general public mentioned above, 70.5 percent of the respondents stated that the opposition assemblymen's party switching was caused by the government's investigation and intimidation tactics aimed at the GNP (*Joongang Ilbo,* September 22, 1998).

18. In a survey of U.S. politicians, businesspersons, and reporters in July 1998, sponsored by the Korean Trade Association, the most frequently cited reason for the lack of American investment in Korea was "political instability caused by the small governing coalition and the large opposition (28.7 percent of the responses given)." Respondents gave this reason more frequently than "the tension between North and South Korea (24.4 percent)," "the exclusive nature of Korean culture, which makes it difficult for foreigners to do business in Korea (14.5 percent)," and "the unstable business-labor relations (9.2 percent)" (*Joongang Ilbo,* July 10, 1998). In a survey of Korean voters on the one hundredth day of the Kim government in June, 83.5 percent of the respondents stated that some sort of political reorganization was necessary. Among them, 49.6 percent said the reorganization should happen through electoral processes in a natural fashion, while 43.7 percent were willing to endorse the NCNP's reorganization attempts before the next national assembly elections (*Joongang Ilbo,* June 6, 1998). Given the country's urgent need to implement economic reform policies based on a stable political system, and from the reactions of both Korean voters and international opinion leaders toward the political situation in Korea in the late 1990s, the Kim Dae-jung government's "reorganization" efforts appeared to

be a low-cost political maneuver. Of the "reforms" stated in this chapter, the only one actually implemented by the Kim government was to reduce the size of the national assembly. For the next national assembly election in 2000, the size was reduced to 273 (from 299). As we will find out, however, the size of the national assembly reverted back to 299 in 2004.

19. Korean voters had traditionally been very generous to incumbents and unwilling to punish them, even after revelations of scandals, financial wrongdoing, or party switching. See chapter 4 for empirical evidence of Korean voters' unwillingness to punish incumbents in previous elections.

20. To mitigate the weaknesses of these electoral systems while taking advantage of their strengths, many countries have adopted an electoral system that mixes the (majority-rule) SMDs and PR. Obviously, Alternatives 3 and 4 fall in this category.

6. Uncertainty in Foreign Policy Making

1. See: international conflict (e.g., Morrow 1989; Fearon 1994a and 1994b; Fearon 1995; Kim and Bueno de Mesquita 1995; Powell 1996; Bueno de Mesquita, Morrow, and Zorick 1997; Wagner 2000; Werner 2000), alliance formation (e.g., Morrow 1994; Smith 1995; Smith 1998), deterrence (e.g., Nalebuff 1991), domestic constraints on foreign policy (e.g., Iida 1993; Fearon 1994a and 1994b; Fearon 1997; Schultz 1998); and reputation building in the world political economy (e.g., Alt, Calvert, and Humes 1988).

2. As readers can see, this chapter deals with the "international" relationships among the United States, South Korea, and North Korea. As I stated in chapter 1, the opening of the relationships between South Korea and North Korea and between the United States and North Korea allowed the emergence of a new issue dimension, changed the direction of political discourse, and fundamentally reshaped the democratic transition in South Korea. Therefore, these changing relationships must be at the core of any discussion of the subsequent democratic transition in Korea. See chapter 1.

3. Another way to interpret the uncertainty about the North Korean preference is the split within the North Korean leadership. That is, even if Kim Jong-il wants to push for true change in North Korea, he may not be able to sustain it without potential loss of power, given the disagreements among top leaders of the communist party and the military about the method and pace of reform (see *Hankuk Ilbo*, December 15, 2000).

4. For previous studies applying game-theoretic models to inter-Korean relations, see Ahn (1995) and Kim (1995), among others.

5. Under the Geneva agreement, North Korea would freeze its graphite-moderated reactor and related facilities and eventually dismantle them. The International Atomic Energy Agency (IAEA) would be allowed to monitor this freeze, and North Korea would provide full cooperation to the IAEA for this

purpose. In return, the United States would undertake arrangements for the provision to North Korea of light-water reactor power plants with a total generating capacity of approximately 2,000 MW by a target date of 2003. In addition, the U.S. would make arrangements to provide alternative energy in the form of heavy oil for heating and electricity production to offset the energy foregone due to the freeze of North Korea's graphite-moderated reactors and related facilities. See further details of the agreement at www.kedo.org/pdfs/AgreedFramework.pdf.

6. Other countries that "made" this list were Cuba, Iran, Iraq, Libya, Sudan, and Syria.

7. From the modeling point of view, an ideal way to analyze the South Korea–North Korea interaction and the U.S.–North Korea interaction together would be to treat these two interactions as nested games in a single model (see Tsebelis 1990). Given the technically complicated nature of these interactions (as in two figures and two appendixes), however, I chose not to incorporate them into a single model here, leaving it as a future research topic.

8. The two leaders further announced that "the North Korean missile development was for a peaceful purpose and did not pose any threat to those countries honoring North Korea's sovereignty." They also emphasized that the 1972 Anti-Ballistic Missile Treaty was the basis of global strategic stability. Obviously, Mr. Putin was using the summit with Kim Jong-il to criticize the Bush administration's concept of missile defense.

9. Lee Hoi-chang had continuously stated his preferences for a North Korean aid policy based on reciprocity. At a meeting of presidential candidates and President Kim Dae-jung on October 23, 2002, after North Korea admitted its nuclear development program, Lee Hoi-chang called for the cessation of all monetary aid to the North that could be subverted to fund its nuclear programs. On the other hand, Roh Mu-hyun advocated continuous cooperation with the North to prevent heightened tension in the Korean peninsula (*Joong-ang Ilbo,* various dates, 2002).

7. A Risky Game to Play

1. The Constitutional Court could refuse to consider the case, uphold it, or overturn the impeachment.

2. Surveys of the electorate throughout the period following the impeachment vote in March leading up to the national assembly elections in April indicated that the GNP would have lost a lot more seats had the elections been held right after the impeachment of President Roh. The mismanagement of the campaign effort on the part of the Woori Party leaders and the fresh image of the new leader of the GNP (a daughter of former President Park Chung-hee) made the contest between the two parties much closer than it would have been otherwise (*Joongang Ilbo,* various dates, 2004).

3. It did not reveal the vote split among its members.

4. CNN.com (May 13, 2004) and *New York Times* (May 14, 2004).

5. The verbal description in this section is based on a more technical equilibrium analysis, which I do not show here. It can be downloaded from the author's Web site at http://heeminkim.net.

8. Concluding Remarks

1. "The POLITY IV" index assigns a score of -5 for 1987 (the POLITY score of -6 and below means autocracy). The period of 1987 to 1989 is considered a "transition" period. It assigns a score of +6 for 1989 through 1998, and then +8 thereafter (the score of +6 and above means democracy). "The Freedom House" index gives South Korea a Political Rights Score of 2, a Civil Liberties Score of 2, and the "Status" of "Free" for 2002. By 2009, the nation had a Political Rights Score of 1, a Civil Liberties Score of 2, and the "Status" of "Free" (countries are ranked on a scale of 1–7, with 1 representing the highest level of freedom and 7 representing the lowest). The Unified Democracy Scores (UDS), a composite scale of democracy developed by Melton, Meserve, and Pemstein and estimated using a Bayesian statistical measurement model, assigns a mean democracy score 0.168265 for 1987, but a near perfect score of 0.910096 for 1999 (http://www.systemicpeace.org/polity/polity4.htm; http://www.freedomhouse.org/template.cfm?page=439; http://www.unified-democracy-scores.org/uds.html).

Bibliography

Sources in English Language

"A Blow to Roh." 1992. *The Economist*, March 28: 31–32.

Ahn Byeonggil. 1995. "Domestic Uncertainty and Coordination between North and South Korea." In *Rationality and Politics in the Korean Peninsula*, ed. Kim HeeMin and Kim Woosang, 119–142. East Lansing: Michigan State University.

Almond, Gabriel A., Russell Dalton, G. Bingham Powell Jr., and Kaare Strom. 2006. *Comparative Politics Today: A World View*, 8th updated ed. New York: Longman.

Alt, James E., Randall L. Calvert, and Brian D. Humes. 1988. "Reputation and Hegemonic Stability: A Game-Theoretic Analysis." *American Political Science Review* 82:445–466.

Axelrod, Robert. 1970. *Conflict of Interest: A Theory of Divergent Goals with Allocations to Politics*. Chicago: Markham Publishing Company.

Barnes, Samuel, et al. 1962. "The German Party System and the 1961 Federal Election." *American Political Science Review* 26:909–910.

Bates, Robert, et al. 1998. *Analytic Narratives*. Princeton: Princeton Univ. Press.

Bates, Robert. 1997a. "Area Studies and the Discipline: A Useful Controversy." *PS* 30:166–170.

———. 1997b. "Comparative Politics and Rational Choice: A Review Essay." *American Political Science Review* 91:699–705.

———. 1989. *Beyond the Miracle of the Market: The Political Economy of Agrarian Development in Kenya*. Cambridge: Cambridge Univ. Press.

———, ed. 1988. *Toward a Political Economy of Development: A Rational Choice Perspective*. Berkeley: Univ. of California Press.

———. 1981. *Markets and States in Tropical Africa*. Berkeley: Univ. of California Press.

Beck, Peter M. 1993. "From Transition to Consolidation: Crafting Democracy in South Korea." Paper presented at the international conference on the "Transformation in the Korean Peninsula Toward the 21st Century," Michigan State University, July.

Black, Duncan. 1958. *Theory of Committees and Elections*. Cambridge: Cambridge Univ. Press.

Bogdanor, Vernon. 1983. "Conclusion: Electoral Systems and Party Systems." In *Democracy and Elections: Electoral Systems and Their Political Consequences*, ed. Vernon Bogdanor and David Butler, 247–262. Cambridge: Cambridge Univ. Press.

Booth, James, et al., eds. 1993. *Politics and Rationality.* Cambridge: Cambridge Univ. Press.

Brady, David, and Mo Jongryn. 1992. "Electoral Systems and Institutional Choice: A Case Study of the 1988 Korean Elections." *Comparative Political Studies* 24:405–429.

Bueno de Mesquita, Bruce, James D. Morrow, and Ethan R. Zorick. 1997. "Capabilities, Perception, and Escalation." *American Political Science Review* 91:15–27.

Burton, Michael, Richard Gunther, and John Higley. 1992. "Introduction: Elite Transformations and Democratic Regimes." In *Elites and Democratic Consolidation in Latin America and Southern Europe,* ed. J. Higley and R. Gunther, 1–37. Cambridge: Cambridge Univ. Press.

Cheng Tun-jen. 1990. "Is the Dog Barking?: The Middle Class and Democratic Movements in the East Asian NICs." *International Study Notes* 15:10–16.

Cheng Tun-jen and Lawrence B. Krause. 1991. "Democracy and Development: With Special Attention to Korea." *Journal of Northeast Asian Studies* 10 (2): 3–25.

Cheng Tun-jen and Tallian Mihae Lim. 1995. "Bargaining over Electoral Reform during the Democratic Transition." In *Rationality and Politics in the Korean Peninsula,* ed. Kim HeeMin and Kim Woosang, 17–52. East Lansing: Michigan State University.

CNN.com, May 13, 2004.

Cohen, Frank S. 1997. "Proportional versus Majoritarian Ethnic Conflict Management in Democracies." *Comparative Political Studies* 30:607–630.

Conradt, David. 1970. "Electoral Law Politics in West Germany." *Political Studies* 18:343–345.

Cotton, James. 1992. "Understanding the State in South Korea: Bureaucratic-Authoritarian or State Autonomy Theory?" *Comparative Political Studies* 24:512–531.

Cox, Gary W. 1997. *Making Votes Count: Strategic Coordination in the World's Electoral Systems.* Cambridge: Cambridge Univ. Press.

Dahl, Robert A. 1971. *Polyarchy: Participation and Opposition.* New Haven: Yale Univ. Press.

Downs, Anthony. 1957. *An Economic Theory of Democracy.* New York: Harper and Row.

Duverger, Maurice. 1951. *Political Parties: Their Organization and Activity in the Modern State.* London: Methuen.

Fearon, James D. 1994a. "Domestic Political Audiences and the Escalation of International Disputes." *American Political Science Review* 88:577–592.

———. 1994b. "Signaling versus the Balance of Power and Interests: An Empirical Test of a Crisis Bargaining Model." *Journal of Conflict Resolution* 38:236–269.

———. 1995. "Rationalist Explanations for War." *International Organization* 49:379–414.

———. 1997. "Signaling Foreign Policy Interests: Tying Hands Versus Sinking Costs." *Journal of Conflict Resolution* 41:68–90.

Fisher, Stephen L. 1973. "The Wasted Vote Theses: West German Evidence." *Comparative Politics* 5 (2): 293–299.

Frank, Robert H. 1990. "Rethinking Rational Choice." In *Beyond the Market Place: Rethinking Economy and Society,* ed. Roger Friedland and A. F. Robertson, 53–87. New York: Aldine de Gruyter.

Friedman, Jeffrey, ed. 1996. *The Rational Choice Controversy.* New Haven: Yale Univ. Press.

Geddes, B. 1991. "A Game Theoretic Model of Reform in Latin American Democracies." *American Political Science Review* 85:371–392.

Geertz, Clifford. 1971. *The Interpretation of Cultures.* New York: Basic Books.

Gerring, John. 2004. "What Is a Case Study and What Is It Good For?" *American Political Science Review* 98:341–354.

Gibbons, Robert. 1992. *Game Theory for Applied Economists.* Princeton: Princeton Univ. Press.

Green, Donald P., and Ian Shapiro. 1994. *Pathologies of Rational Choice Theory.* New Haven: Yale Univ. Press.

Gudgin, Graham, and Peter James Taylor. 1979. *Seats, Votes, and the Spatial Organization of Elections.* London: Pion.

Hamburger, Henry. 1979. *Games as Models of Social Phenomena.* New York: Freeman.

Han Sung-joo. 1990. "South Korea: Politics in Transition." In *Politics in Developing Countries: Comparing Experiences with Democracy,* ed. L. Diamond, J. J. Linz, and S. M. Lipset, 313–350. Boulder: Lynne Rienner Publishers.

http://www.unified-democracy-scores.org/uds.html.

http://www.freedomhouse.org/template.cfm?page=439.

http://www.systemicpeace.org/polity/polity4.htm.

Huntington, Samuel P. 1984. "Will More Countries Become Democratic?" *Political Science Quarterly* 99:193–218.

Iida Keisuke. 1993. "When and How Do Domestic Constraints Matter?" *Journal of Conflict Resolution* 37:403–426.

International Herald Tribune, November 11, 1987, July 29, 2001.

Johnson, Chalmers. 1997. "Perception vs. Observation, or the Contributions of Rational Choice Theory and Area Studies to Contemporary Political Science." *PS* 30:170–175.

Kihl Young Whan. 1988. "South Korea's Search for a New Order: An Overview." In *Political Change in South Korea,* ed. Kim I. P. and Kihl Y. W., 3–21. New York: Korean PWPA.

Kim HeeMin. 2006. "A Risky Game to Play: The Politics of the Impeachment Game in Korea." *East and West Studies* 18:127–149.

———. 2000. "Rational Actors and Institutional Choices in Korea." *Pacific Focus* 15:73–94.

———. 1997. "Rational Choice Theory and Third World Politics: A Case Study of the 1990 Party Merger in Korea." *Comparative Politics* 30:83–100.

———. 1994. "A Theory of Government-Driven Democratization: The Case of Korea." *World Affairs* 156:130–140.

———. 1992. "Kims' Dilemma and the Politics of Rivalry: An Analysis of the 1987 Presidential Election in Korea." *Pacific Focus* 7:141–159.

Kim HeeMin and Choi Jun Y. 2002. "Uncertainty in Foreign Policy Making: A Bayesian Game-Theoretic Analysis of Korea." *Global Economic Review* 31:25–40.

Kim HeeMin and Kim Woosang, eds. 1995. *Rationality and Politics in the Korean Peninsula.* East Lansing: Michigan State University.

Kim HeeMin, G. Bingham Powell Jr., and Richard C. Fording. 2010. "Electoral Systems, Party Systems, and Ideological Representation: An Analysis of Distortion in Western Democracies." *Comparative Politics* 42:167–185.

Kim Woosang. 1995. "South Korea's Foreign Policy Strategies toward Main Actors in the Northeast Asia." In *Rationality and Politics in the Korean Peninsula,* ed. HeeMin Kim and Kim Woosang, 101–118. East Lansing: Michigan State University.

Kim Woosang and Bruce Bueno de Mesquita. 1995. "How Perceptions Influence the Risk of War." *International Studies Quarterly* 39:51–65.

Kitschelt, Herbert. 1994. *The Transformation of European Social Democracy.* New York: Cambridge Univ. Press.

Kitzinger, Uwe W. 1960. *German Electoral Politics.* Oxford: Clarendon Press.

Korea Focus, March–April, May–June 2002.

Kostadinova, Tatiana. 1999. "Mixed Electoral Systems: Determinants and Political Consequences." Ph.D. diss., Florida State University.

Lee Dong Ok and Stanley D. Brunn. 1993. "(Re-)making of Regions in Korean Politics: An Analysis of Recent Presidential Elections." Unpublished manuscript, University of Kentucky, Lexington, Kentucky.

Lee Manwoo. 1990. *The Odyssey of Korean Democracy.* New York: Praeger.

Liao Tim Futing. 1994. *Interpreting Probability Models: Logit, Probit, and Other Generalized Linear Models.* Thousands Oaks, Calif.: SAGE Publications.

Lijphart, Arend. 1994. *Electoral Systems and Party Systems: A Study of Twenty Seven Democracies, 1945–1980.* London: Oxford Univ. Press.

———. 1990. "The Political Consequences of Electoral Laws, 1945–85." *American Political Science Review* 84:481–496.

Lipset, Seymour Martin, and Stein Rokkan. 1967. *Party System and Voter Alignments: Cross-National Perspectives.* New York: Free Press.

Little, Daniel. 1991. "Rational Choice Models and Asian Studies." *Journal of Asian Studies* 50:35–52.

Long, J. Scott. 1997. *Regression Models for Categorical and Limited Dependent Variables.* Thousands Oaks, Calif.: SAGE Publications.

Los Angeles Times, March 8, 2001.

Lustick, Ian S. 1997. "The Disciplines of Political Science and Studying the Culture of Rational Choice as a Case in Point." *PS* 30:175–179.

McDonald, Michael, and Ian Budge. 2005. *Elections, Parties, Democracy: Conferring the Median Mandate.* New York: Oxford Univ. Press.

Moon Chung-In. 1988. "The Demise of a Developmentalist State?: Neoconservative Reforms and Political Consequences in South Korea." *Journal of Developing Societies* 4:67–84.

Morrow, James D. 1994. "Alliances, Credibility, and Peacetime Costs." *Journal of Conflict Resolution* 38:270–297.

———. 1994. *Game Theory for Political Scientists.* Princeton: Princeton Univ. Press.

———. 1989. "Capabilities, Uncertainty, and Resolve: A Limited Information Model of Crisis Bargaining." *American Journal of Political Science* 33:941–972.

Nalebuff, Barry. 1991. "Rational Deterrence in an Imperfect World." *World Politics* 43:313–335.

New York Times, October 15, 2000, May 14, 2004.

O'Donnell, Guillermo, and Philippe C. Schmitter. 1986. "Tentative Conclusions about Uncertain Democracies." In *Transitions from Authoritarian Rule: Prospects for Democracy,* ed. G. O'Donnell, P. C. Schmitter, and L. Whitehead, 320–345. Baltimore: Johns Hopkins Univ. Press.

Ordeshook, Peter. 1986. *Game Theory and Political Theory.* Cambridge: Cambridge Univ. Press.

Palfrey, Thomas R. 1989. "A Mathematical Proof of Duverger's Law." In *Models of Strategic Choice in Politics,* ed. Peter Ordeshook, 121–130. Ann Arbor: Univ. of Michigan Press.

Park Jin. 1990. "Political Change in South Korea: The Challenge of the Conservative Alliance." *Asian Survey* 30:1154–1168.

Polanyi, Karl. 1957. *The Great Transformation.* Boston: Beacon Press.

Popkin, Samuel. 1991. *The Reasoning Voters.* Chicago: Univ. of Chicago Press.

———. 1979. *The Rational Peasant: The Political Economy of Rural Society in Vietnam.* Berkeley: Univ. of California Press.

Powell, Robert. 1996. "Uncertainty, Shifting Power, and Appeasement." *American Political Science Review* 90:749–764.

Przeworski, Adam. 1992. "The Games of Transition." In *Issues in Democratic Consolidation: The New South American Democracies in Comparative Perspective,* ed. S. Mainwaring, G. O'Donnell, and J. S. Valenzuela, 109–132. Notre Dame, Ind.: Notre Dame Univ. Press.

Rae, Douglas W. 1967. *The Political Consequences of Electoral Laws.* New Haven: Yale Univ. Press.

Rae, Douglas W., and Michael Taylor. 1970. *The Analysis of Political Cleavages.* New Haven: Yale Univ. Press.

Riker, William H. 1982. "The Two Party System and Duverger's Law." *American Political Science Review* 76:753–766.

———. 1962. *The Theory of Political Coalition.* New Haven: Yale Univ. Press.

Rustow, Dankwart A. 1970. "Transitions to Democracy: Toward a Dynamic Model." *Comparative Politics* 2:337–364.

Sartori, Giovanni. 1997. *Comparative Constitutional Engineering: An Inquiry into Structures, Incentives, and Outcomes.* New York: New York Univ. Press.

Schattschneider, Elmer E. 1960. *The Semisovereign People.* Forth Worth: HBJ College Publishers.

Schofield, Norman, Bernard Grofman, and Scott L. Feld. 1988. "The Core and the Stability of Group Choice in Spatial Voting Games." *American Political Science Review* 82:195–211.

Schultz, Kenneth A. 1998. "Domestic Opposition and Signaling in International Crises." *American Political Science Review* 92:829–844.

Smith, Alastair. 1998. "Extended Deterrence and Alliance Formation." *International Interactions* 24:315–343.

———. 1995. "Alliance Formation and War." *International Studies Quarterly* 39:405–425.

Sohn Hak-Kyu. 1989. *Authoritarianism and Opposition in South Korea.* London: Routledge.

Taagepera, Rein, and Matthew S. Shugart. 1989. *Seats and Votes: The Effects and Determinants of Electoral Systems.* New Haven: Yale Univ. Press.

Tsebelis, George. 1990. *Nested Games.* Berkeley: Univ. of California Press.

Valenzuela, J. Samuel. 1992. "Democratic Consolidation in Post-Transitional Settings: Notion, Process and Facilitating Conditions." In *Issues in Democratic Consolidation: The New South American Democracies in Comparative Perspective,* ed. S. Mainwaring, G. O'Donnell, and J. S. Valenzuela, 2–43. Notre Dame, Ind.: Notre Dame Univ. Press.

van Winden, Frans A.A.M. 1988. "The Economic Theory of Political Decision Making: A Survey and Perspective." In *Public Choice,* ed. Julien van den Broeck, 121–145. Boston: Kluwer Academic Publishers.

Vowles, Jack. 1995. "The Politics of Electoral Reform in New Zealand." *International Political Science Review* 16:95–115.

Wagner, R. Harrison. 2000. "Bargaining and War." *American Journal of Political Science* 44:469–484.

Washington Post, June 7, 2001.

Werner, Suzanne. 2000. "Deterring Intervention: The Stakes of War and Third-Party Involvement." *American Journal of Political Science* 44:720–732.

Sources in Korean Language

"The Agitating 80s." A Special Series. Munhwa Broadcasting Company. 1990.

Ahn Gyung-hwan. 1990. "Comments on Korean Domestic Politics." *Wolgan Chosun* (December): 124–136.

Cha Jong Chun. 1988. "Voters Choices among the Candidates of the 1987 Presidential Election." *The Korean Journal of Sociology* 22:143–159.

Cho Jinman. 2001. "An Analytical Review of Civil Influence Over the 16th General Election in Korea." *Yonsei Journal of Social Science* 7:167–194.

Cho Kisuk. 2003. "Policy and Political Party in Korea." In *Understanding of the Contemporary Party Politics*, ed. Sim Jiyeon, 68–91. Seoul: Baek San Press.

———. 2000. *Regional Voting and Rational Voters*. Seoul: Nanam.

Cho Kisuk and Kim Sun Woong. 2002. "Did Blackballing by the Citizens Alliance Lower Voter Turnout in South Korea's 2000 National Assembly Elections?" *The Korean Political Science Review* 36:163–183.

Cho Y. J. 1993. "Jin-san Was a Real Political Giant with Many Personal Proteges." *Sisa Journal* (May): 210–231.

Choi Hansoo. 1995. "What Determines the 6.27 Local Election?: Partisanship and Regionalism." *Korean Political Science Review* 29:141–161.

Choi Jang Jip. 2002. *Democracy after Democracy: The Origin and Crisis of Conservative Democracy in Korea*. Seoul: Humanitas.

Chosun Ilbo [*Chosun Daily News*], July 23, 1999.

Chung Jinmin. 1993. "Generational Gap and the Korean Elections." In *The Korean Election I*, ed. Lee Nam Young, 83–102. Seoul: Nanam.

Dong-a Ilbo, January 23, 1990, December 19, 1992.

Han Dong-yun. 1990. "The Three-Party Merger and the Secret Agreement among Roh Tae-woo, Kim Young-sam, and Kim Jong-pil." *Shin Dong-a* (March): 190–210.

Han Myung-kyu. 1990. "Is Opposition Alliance Possible?" *Shin Dong-a* (March): 168–181.

Hankuk Ilbo [*The Korea Daily News*], March 26, 1992, September 28, 1999, various dates, 2000, 2001, and 2004.

Jang Young-sup. 1990. "Roh and Kim, Honeymoon or Conflict?" *Wolgan Chosun* (December): 99–121.

Joongang Ilbo [*Central Daily News*], various dates, 1998, 1999, 2001, 2002, 2004.

Kang Won-taek. 2004. "Impeachment Issue and the 17th National Assembly Elections." Paper presented at the Korean Political Science Association. Seoul, August 28–30.

———. 2003. *Electoral Politics in South Korea: Ideology, Region, Generation, and Media*. Seoul: Purungil.

———. 2002. "Generation, Ideology, and the Rho Moo-hyun Phenomenon." *Kekansasang* 14: 80–102.

Kim Chang-gi. 1992. "Kim Duk-yong Who Became a Top Political Aide for a Former Enemy." *Wolgan Chosun* (August): 540–558.

Kim Jae-hong and Choong-shik Kim. 1990. "Four Parties' Strategy of Breaking the Four-Party System." *Shin Dong-a* (February): 201–230.

Kwon Young-ki. 1990. "Kim Young-sam and Park Chul-eon, Friends or Enemies?" *Wolgan Chosun* (April): 97–121.

Lee Gang-shik. 1970. "The Beginning and the End of the Presidential Candidate Nominating Convention of the New Democratic Party." *Shin Dong-a* (November): 84–93.

Lee Jun Han and Leem Kyung Hoon. 2004. "The 2004 National Assembly Election: A Critical Election?" *Journal of Korean Politics* 13:117–141.

Lee Jungbok. 1992. "Voting Behavior of the Korean Electorates in the 14th National Assembly Elections." *Korean Political Science Review* 26:113–132.

Lee Kapyoon. 1999. *The Korean Elections and Regionalism*. Seoul: Orum.

Lee Nam Young. 1999. "The 1998 Local Election and Regionalism." In *The Korean Election III: The 1998 Local Election*, ed. Cho Jungbin. Seoul: Purungil.

———. 1998. "Regionalism and Voting Behavior in the Korean Electorates." In *The Korean Election II: The 15th Presidential Election*, ed. Lee Nam Young, 48–71. Seoul: Purungil.

Lee Sang-woo. 1992. "From a Fighter to a Moderate." *Shin Dong-a* (July): 148–160.

Lee Sookjong. 1996. "Political Orientation and Voting Behavior." In *Evaluations on the 15th National Assembly Elections*, ed. Sejong Institution, 120–152. Sungnam: Sejong Institution Press.

Lee Young-suk. 1992. "A Born Gambler Who Controls the Change of Events." *Shin Dong-a* (July): 136–147.

Park Chan-jong. 1992. "The Reason Why Any One of the Two Kims and One Chung Should Not Become the President." *Shin Dong-a* (July): 210–219.

Park Chan Wook. 1993. "Party Votes in the 14th National Assembly Elections." In *The Korean Election I*, ed. Lee Nam Young, 24–41. Seoul: Nanam.

Sisa Journal, February 4, 1990.

Sohn Ho Chul. 1995. *Contemporary Korean Politics: Theory and History*. Seoul: Social Critique.

Yonhap News, March 17, 2004, August 10, 2009.

Index

www.ingramcontent.com/pod-product-compliance
Lightning Source LLC
Chambersburg PA
CBHW031536260326
41914CB00032B/1830/J